A General Introduction to the Series

THIS series has been undertaken in the conviction that there can be no subject of study more important than history. Great as have been the conquests of natural science in our time—such that many think of ours as a scientific age *par excellence*—it is even more urgent and necessary that advances should be made in the social sciences if we are to gain control of the forces of nature loosed upon us. The bed out of which all the social sciences spring is history; there they find, in greater or lesser degree, subject-matter and material, verification or contradiction.

There is no end to what we can learn from history if only we will, for it is coterminous with life. Its special field is the life of man in society, and at every point we can learn vicariously from the experience of others before us in history.

To take one point only—the understanding of politics: how can we hope to understand the world of affairs around us if we do not know how it came to be what it is? How to understand Germany, or Soviet Russia, or the United States—or ourselves—without knowing something of their history?

There is no subject that is more useful, or indeed indispensable.

Some evidence of the growing awareness of this may be seen in the immense increase in the interest of the reading public in history, and the much larger place the subject has come to take in education in our time.

This series has been planned to meet the needs and demands of a very wide public and of education—they are indeed the same. I am convinced that the most congenial, as well as the most concrete and practical, approach to history is the biographical, through the lives of the great men whose actions have been so much part of history, and whose careers in turn have been so moulded and formed by events.

The key idea of this series, and what distinguishes it from any other that has appeared, is the intention by way of a biography of a great man to open up a significant historical theme; for example, Cromwell and the Puritan Revolution, or Lenin and the Russian Revolution.

My hope is, in the end, as the series fills out and completes itself, by a sufficient number of biographies to cover whole periods and subjects in that way. To give you the history of the United States, for example, or the British Empire or France, *via* a number of biographies of their leading historical figures.

That should be something new, as well as convenient and practical, in education.

I need hardly say that I am a strong believer in people with good academic standards writing once more for the general reading public, and of the public being given the best that the universities can provide. From this point of view this series is intended to bring the university into the homes of the people.

A. L. ROWSE.

ALL SOULS COLLEGE,
    OXFORD.

Contents

FOR
PERKINS AND ROB
AND MY FRIENDS OF
ALBEMARLE AND FAIRFAX

Chapter One

Early Life (1732—1748)

GEORGE WASHINGTON was born at Wakefield on the Potomac River on 11th February 1731 (Old Style), 22nd February 1732 (New Style). Though February 22nd later became the "official" birthday, Washington himself often celebrated on the 11th, or, on occasion, on both. He was the third son of Augustine Washington, but the first child by his second wife, Mary Ball. On both sides of his family, Washington could claim "Cavalier" descent. His great-grandfather, John Washington, had been driven from England because of the sufferings inflicted by the Puritans on his father, the Reverend Lawrence Washington, a "Scandalous, Malignant Priest", "a common frequenter of Alehouses". Other members of the family served the Stuarts, and one held Worcester for the King for a few months in 1646. His mother, Mary Ball, much younger than her husband and socially his inferior, was an orphaned daughter of another fortune-seeker whose parents had left England during the Commonwealth.

The Washington plantation, in Westmoreland County, covering 1,000 acres and extending for a mile along the Potomac between Bridges Creek and Pope's Creek, was much smaller than its counterparts on the James and the Rappahannock Rivers, the tobacco highways. The planters on the lower and middle Potomac were a generation behind those to the south, a generation nearer the western wilderness. Washington's birthplace lacked the elegance of Westover and Shirley on the James: it was a comfortable but unpretentious one-storey-and-a-half brick house, with dormer windows and double outside chimneys.

In 1735, Augustine Washington moved to a plantation on Hunting Creek (the later Mount Vernon), and then in 1738 to a third, River or Ferry Farm, on a bluff on the Rappahannock overlooking Fredericksburg, where, suddenly in 1743, he died, of a frequent ailment of the day, "gout of the stomack". He was, physically, tall and strong, vigorous and restless. He was a Justice of the Peace and a Sheriff. He was a land-owner on a considerable though not, by Virginian standards, a major scale : he had increased his holdings from 1,700 acres at the time of his first marriage to 10,000 at his death.

On his death, Lawrence, the eldest son, inherited the largest share of the estate—the Hunting Creek lands; Augustine, the second son, got the lands in Westmoreland County; George and his mother received the Ferry Farm, four other lots, ten slaves and a reversionary interest in Hunting Creek should Lawrence die without children. Ferry Farm was a modest estate, a wooden house of eight medium-sized rooms, standing in some 260 acres of not very fertile land. For a junior member of a large family, whose two eldest brothers had had an education much superior to his own, there was little promise here of wealth or distinction.

It is around Washington's childhood that the legends are most thickly clustered and where the evidence is thinnest. Clearly he was greatly impressed by Hunting Creek, where he spent his years from three to six and which retained a permanent grip on his affections; Mount Vernon, as it was to become, with its magnificent view over the stately Potomac, was always to him "home". Most of his childhood was spent at Ferry Farm (1738–43). If he ever threw a Spanish silver dollar across a river or chopped down a cherry-tree, Ferry Farm was the place where he did it. Here, or in the vicinity, he was educated. His two half-brothers, like his father, had been educated at the Appleby school in the English Lake District, but George did not have this good fortune; either the family finances did not allow it (for which there is no evidence), or his father's death prevented it, or his mother did not want him to leave home. The Rev. Jonathan Boucher, who was in 1759–62 tutor to Washington's stepson "Jacky" Custis, and who later became an embittered Loyalist, wrote that Washington in his youth "had no other education than reading, writing and accounts, which he was taught by a convict servant whom his father brought over for a school-teacher". Other traditions put Washington at schools in Fredericksburg or in Westmoreland County.

What evidence there is indicates a robust and vigorous youth, groping at Latin—or copying another's—but never learning French; writing adolescent love poetry; practising and perfecting a legible, neat and characteristic hand; practising and failing, then, as throughout life, to perfect his spelling; addicted to mathematics and interested very early in the problems of surveying the land as an outlet for his skill in measuring and computing. His training was not intellectual, and he did not appear to take much interest in ideas, as did Jefferson or Madison or his near neighbour George Mason. At Ferry Farm there was an acceptance of belief in God, but apparently no burning religious zeal. Though his later correspondence shows some knowledge of Pope, Addison and the Bible, and *Tom Jones* and *Humphry Clinker* were apparently on his shelves, his account-books indicate a farmer's and a soldier's taste. He was greatly impressed by Addison's *Cato*, but in the years before the Revolution, the book to which he seems to have devoted most attention was Duhamel's *Practical Treatise of Husbandry*.

His tastes were—and remained—practical; he was probably a leader as a boy less by reason of his mental gifts than by his physical prowess—to that extent there may be a kernel of truth in the legends of "Parson" Weems. Later observers commented repeatedly on his height, his big feet, his freakishly large and strong hands—hands, said Lafayette, "the largest I have ever seen on a human being"—his superb horsemanship. If these things produced a reliance on his physical strength and a taste for battle—"I was strongly bent to arms"—which the Indian frontier, the French wars and half-brother Lawrence's conversation stirred, they gave him also a rare and valuable confidence in himself and in his changing environment, a confidence that his more bookish compatriots often lacked.

One product of his schooldays has remained—Washington's "Rules of Civility". These boyish manuscripts of his fourteenth year were first published in 1888, and believed to be largely his own composition. They follow closely a Jesuit work, published in a French translation in 1617, or they may have been inspired by a translation by Francis Hawkins in 1640 of a similar French book on conduct, *Youth's Behaviour or Decencie in Conversation amongst Men*. They consist of a hundred or more maxims of behaviour, highly platitudinous no doubt, but suggesting that the tact, the genuine consideration for others and the grave good manners of the later man were carefully cultivated in youth, not in a foreign finishing school with easy informality but soberly and by rote. Washington learnt his code of conduct carefully, perhaps pedantically, and he never found it easy to relax under it. Dignity came naturally, graciousness less easily. And again, though the code had its preachments— "Let your Recreations be Manfull not Sinfull"—they were of practice not of doctrine :

"EVERY Action done in Company, ought to be with Some Sign of Respect, to those that are Present.

"Shew Nothing to your Friend that may affright him.

"In the Presence of Others sing not to yourself with a humming Noise, nor Drum with your fingers or feet.

"When you see a Crime punished, you may be inwardly Pleased; but always show Pity to the Suffering Offender.

"When in Company, put not your Hands to any Part of the Body, not usualy Discovered.

"SHAKE not the head, Feet or Legs, rowl not the Eyes, lift not one eyebrow higher than the other, wry not the mouth, and bedew no mans face with your Spittle, by approaching too near him when you speak.

"Being to advise or reprehend any one, consider whether it ought to be in publick or in Private; presently, or at some other time in what terms to do it & in reproving Shew no Signs of Cholar but do it with all Sweetness and Mildness.

"Play not the Peacock."

The two major influences on the young Washington were not tutors but people very close to him indeed : his mother, Mary Ball Washington, and his half-brother Lawrence. According to the account of a cousin in George Washington Parke Custis' somewhat suspect *Recollections*, published in 1860, Washington's mother was an awesome person—"I have often been present with her sons, proper tall fellows, too, and we were all as mute as mice". She appears to have been strict, querulous, poorly educated and high-tempered, addicted to managing but not very skilful at it. On her husband's death in 1743 she sent George to live with his half-brother Augustine at Wakefield, and stayed on herself at Ferry Farm. When Augustine and Lawrence planned to send George to sea, the strong-minded mother got wind of the scheme, abruptly brought George back to Ferry Farm and sent him to school in Fredericksburg. She consulted a half-brother in London, Joseph Ball, on the wisdom of her son's going to sea, and his blunt advice from Stratford-by-Bow reinforced her strong motherly instincts :

"I think he had better be put aprentice to a tinker . . . for they will . . . cut him and staple him and use him like a Negro, or rather, like a dog. And as for any considerable preferment in the Navy, it is not to be expected, there are always too many grasping for it here, who have interest and he has none. And if he should get to be master of a Virginia ship (which will be very difficult to do) a planter that has three or four hundred acres of land and three or four slaves, if he be industrious, may live more comfortably, and leave his family in better Bread, than such a master of a ship can. . . . He must not be hasty to be rich; but must go on gently and with patience as things will naturally go. This method, without aiming at being a fine gentleman before his time, will carry a man more surely, and comfortably, through the World, than going to sea."

After 1748, when George went to live with Lawrence at Hunting Creek, the relationship between mother and son appears to have become cool. Of Washington's letters to his mother, beginning in the formal fashion of his age "Honour'd Madam" and ending "Your Most Affect. and Dutiful Son", only six survive; four of these were written in 1755, and there is not one extant between October 1757 and February 1787. She does not seem often—if, indeed, ever—to have visited him when he became master of Mount Vernon, and he appears actively to have discouraged her from doing so. He said his house resembled a "well-resorted tavern".

"This would, were you to be an inhabitant of it oblige you to do one of 3 things : 1st to be always dressing to appear in company; 2d, to come . . . in a dishabille, or 3d to be as a prisoner in your bed-chamber. The first you'ld not like, . . . the Second I should not like, . . . And the 3d, . . . would not be pleasing to either of us."

So she continued to live at Ferry Farm until 1772, and thereafter near her daughter in Fredericksburg. Later she became a source of anxiety to her son, as she complained of being neglected and of not having enough money to meet her needs, despite his generosity. This led to a movement in the Virginian Assembly to grant her a pension, a proceeding Washington tried to stop. He resented the imputation of being an "unjust and undutifull son". She died in 1789, a few months after his inauguration as President. But about her, too—even more erroneously than about him and with much less warrant—the legends have gathered. The tale is still told in Fredericksburg that, in the thick of the Revolutionary War, Mary Washington said she was sure that "I shall hear some day that they have hung George".

Lawrence was a much more attractive figure, and throughout his life remained a hero to his half-brother. He was fourteen years older than George, and returned from his schooling in England when George was six. He was urbane, accomplished and studious. He served with the Colonial troops (mainly convicts) raised to help—or, as it proved, to hinder—Admiral Vernon in the unsuccessful and costly attack on Cartagena in 1741. He returned from that inglorious affair with a prestige in arms that was quite unmerited but which won him the post of Adjutant of Virginia, and perhaps with the beginnings of the tuberculosis that killed him twelve years later.

On his father's death in 1743, Lawrence inherited the Hunting Creek property and married Anne, the spirited daughter of his neighbour across the stream, Colonel William Fairfax of Belvoir, cousin and agent of Thomas, Lord Fairfax, who owned the vast Northern Neck proprietary—the lands between the Potomac and the Rappahannock stretching towards the unmapped West. Lawrence Washington proceeded to build a house for his bride, and called it Mount Vernon in a hero-worship of his own. Their children all died in infancy. To Mount Vernon, therefore, in 1748 came George as heir to live, a tall, powerfully built, athletic young man, blue-eyed and softly spoken, proud and self-contained in manner, and at first out of place in the elegant world of the Fairfaxes. Here he struck up a friendship with Colonel Fairfax's son, George William, and with Sally and Mary Cary. Here there was added to his thin academic equipment some knowledge of that great world hinted at in his rules of civility.

And from the summer of 1747 there was at Belvoir another figure, perhaps even then more important in his eyes —for he was little touched by romance at any point in his career—than any "Lowland Beauty" whom he might salute in verse, or any Sally Fairfax to whom he might occasionally write somewhat indiscreet letters. This figure was the Proprietor himself, the sixth Lord Fairfax, come to survey his five-million-acre holding on both sides of the Blue Ridge. For a tough young man, skilled at surveying, with an instinctive love of the land and a masterful wish to be owner of it, brought up amid the rumours of French and Spanish and Indian wars, this seemed opportunity indeed.

Chapter Two

Surveyor and Colonel:
The Virginian Frontier (1748—1758)

IN 1748 the Virginia Tidewater, extending to the limits of
navigation at the fall-line of the rivers and covering an
area the size of England, was well settled. Here lived the
great majority of the colony's population, estimated at
80,000. Here had been developed in the seventeenth century
an unusual economy, dependent on deep, slow-moving, tidal
rivers like the James and the York, the Potomac and the Rappahannock, "the stream that comes and goes", on cheap land
and labour and on a staple crop, tobacco. Tobacco was
both exportable wealth and currency in the colony; the
plantation was the economic unit and the big house the social
centre. There were in 1750 only eight towns, and most of
them were "little better than inconsiderable villages". Difficulty of communication put a premium on hospitality; early
death, frequent remarriage and large families made kinship
as important as it was involved; life was abundant and
gracious in the Tidewater.

West of the fall-line lay the rolling piedmont, a frontier
still in process of settlement, and still farther west a world
that was mountainous and marginal, legendary and little
explored, the land of the "Western Waters". There was great
uncertainty about its resources, its geography and its ownership. There was controversy with other colonies—North
Carolina, Maryland and Pennsylvania—over mutual boundaries, and the dream died hard of a short-cut through it to
the Indian sea, with wealth of furs and precious stones *en
route*. Yet even at the time Robert Beverley wrote his history, in 1705, one dream was being replaced by another: of
virgin land to be occupied by those with the resources to

reach it and those endowed with energy and courage. Beverley described his fellow Virginians as "not minding anything but to be masters of great tracts of land—lords of vast territory". The exotic cavalcade led in 1716 by Lieutenant-Governor Spotswood over the Blue Ridge into the fertile and lovely Valley of Virginia, the "knights of the Golden Horseshoe", was recruited largely from Tidewater planters. The great families acquired huge holdings, their motive less settlement than speculation.

Despite the grasping hands of Byrds, Beverleys, Carters, Spotswoods and Randolphs, the Shenandoah and other valleys began to fill up also with German and Scotch-Irish families, largely from Pennsylvania. By 1776 these were to give a new character to the Appalachian frontier : democratic, strongly religious, industrious, self-reliant, prone to dissent in Church and State, they were to be "the cutting edge of the frontier".

There were three serious obstacles to frontier settlement: moving and warring Indians, the doubt about the extent of the Fairfax holdings in the Valley and, hanging over all, the threat of French control of a line of forts beyond the mountains which might confine the British settlements to the coastal plain. The Indians were the least of these, since the Treaty of Albany, 1722, and further parleys in 1744 between the Five Nations and representatives of Virginia and Maryland, excluded them from the Valley. But to whom did the northern half of it belong—the colony or the Proprietor?

The original grant of the Northern Neck, made to his favourites by Charles I, had come to the sixth Lord Fairfax. It covered the area between the Potomac and the Rappahannock, to the "head springs" of the two rivers. Governor and Council claimed that its western limit extended from the forks of the Rappahannock to the junction of the Shenandoah and the Potomac, giving the proprietary an area of one and a half million acres. Fairfax's own claim, that his boundary ran from the headwaters of the Rapidan to the "head springs" of the Potomac in the mountains west of the Alleghenies, gave him an area of well over five million acres, almost one-quarter of the whole colony.

Fairfax proved a skilful negotiator and, still less usual, an interested Proprietor. He visited the Northern Neck himself in 1737, and then petitioned the Privy Council to determine the area of his estate. The manœuvres were long and dexterous, but he was rewarded in April 1745 with their approval of his case. His success pushed the frontier westward and encouraged further advances on its new perimeter. Enterprising and daring men now looked beyond the Valley of Virginia to the Ohio and to the Mississippi itself. The triumphant return of the Proprietor to Belvoir in 1747 was a decisive event in Washington's life. Through him he gained his first piece of practical experience and his first journey to the West.

In 1748 a surveying expedition was sent to the remote South Branch of the Potomac. The two young men of Belvoir and Mount Vernon, George William Fairfax and George Washington, were given permission to go as observers and assistants. This trip brought Washington very close in friendship to Fairfax, soon to be the husband of Sally Cary—the "Mr. Fairfax" of the Diaries. But it was also a most valuable experience for a young man with an eye for land and business. A surveyor was valued not only for his skill but for his discretion : suitably rewarded, he need not report the true acreage of unoccupied lands held by the planters. He could make money and he could make influential friends. Washington did both. This was an age in which the surveyor was explorer and real estate expert rolled into one, a key figure in land and boundary disputes, and often enough a speculator in his own way—agent, in fact, of the first great entrepreneurial movement in American history.

Washington's account of this six-weeks' "Journey Over the Mountains" is for the most part a bald narrative, in which the phrase "Nothing remarkable happen'd" occurs repeatedly. There are no lyrical descriptions of the Valley as it unfolded below them at Ashby's Gap; there is the shock of a bed at Isaac Pennington's "without Sheets or anything else but only one threadbare blanket, with double its weight of vermin, such as lice, fleas, etc."; there was his first contact with Indians, "Coming from War with only one Scalp", and he saw how amenable they were when liquor "elevated there Spirits". As with many of his diaries, the journal is an account-book first and last, for if he was assiduous in his duties, he does not appear to have enjoyed the work so much as the profits it brought. The people in the Valley, predominantly "Dutch", he regarded as "a parcel of barbarians . . . an uncouth set of people"; of his life among them "there's nothing would make it pass off tolerably but a good reward". And the rewards were good; he had 1,500 acres within a year.

This progress was halted by Lawrence's increasing ill-health. The two brothers tried Berkeley Springs, a primitive health resort on the frontier, to no avail, and in September 1751 they sailed together to see what effect the balmy climate of Barbados would have on Lawrence. It was to be George Washington's only sea voyage, and it was unsuccessful : Lawrence found no cure, and went on alone four months later to the Bermudas, and George himself "was strongly attacked" with smallpox. He carried some traces of its ravages all his life, but it gave him an immunity which was to be valuable later. Lawrence returned to Mount Vernon to die, in June 1752. He left his wife, Anne, a life interest in the estate, with reversion to his only child, a baby, Sarah. If Sarah died without issue, Mount Vernon was to go to "his beloved brother George".

This development transformed Washington's status. From being the all but disinherited younger son of a second marriage, he had become heir to, and in 1761, following the deaths of Sarah and Anne, owner of a large estate; he had travelled abroad and lived sufficiently long in the vicinity of the Fairfaxes to have acquired a certain poise, though his shyness, particularly with women, never left him. Through his brother and the Fairfaxes he had become known to the new Governor of Virginia, Dinwiddie, on whom he had called on his return from Barbados—a significant event, since Dinwiddie, a former Surveyor-General of the Southern Colonies, was himself a shrewd man of business and convinced of the importance of the frontier—and of future wars over it. He was strong, immune from smallpox, shrewd, ambitious, enterprising and rigorously self-disciplined.

Lawrence's death also left vacant the office of Adjutant of the Colony, to which the younger brother aspired. He had never served as a soldier, but he was from the beginning interested in military affairs, and Lawrence's experiences in Cartagena and as Adjutant fired his imagination. Now, however, Virginia was divided into four districts, and George was first allotted the Southern, a vast region extending between the James River and the North Carolina boundary. It brought £100 a year, experience in a new country and in command of men, and the title of Major. A year later, not yet twenty-one, he was transferred to the Northern Neck.

Washington took up his district militia appointment and his work as a surveyor at a moment of increasing political tension. The Treaty of Lancaster with the Indians in 1744 and the ending of the uncertainty over the extent of the Fairfax grant in 1745 had provoked a new interest in the lands beyond the Alleghenies. In 1749 the Ohio Company had received a grant from the Crown of 200,000 acres, with more to follow if the terms attached to the grant were executed—particularly if a fort were built and one hundred families settled on the land within seven years. Among the original members of the Company were Thomas Lee, the father of sons who made history, the Fairfaxes, Lawrence Washington and other Northern Neck landowners—with the Duke of Bedford and John Hanbury acting as their agents in London. Their objectives were both commercial and imperialistic : a fort-cum-trading-post to secure the frontier against French infiltrations from Canada, and to win trade with the Indians. The ideal site for such a base, to be supplied from the upper Potomac, was at the forks of the Ohio, where the Allegheny and Monongahela rivers meet.

These developments revived the frontier clash with France, part of the long struggle between Britain and France in Europe and across the world. The Treaty of Aix-la-Chapelle (1748) had just been signed in Europe, ending the War of the Austrian Succession, but the conflict in the New World had little to do with the conflict in the Old. The colonial wars had an initiative of their own and significantly different titles : the War of the Austrian Succession was known as King George's War, the Seven Years War as the French and Indian War.[1] They were apt, too, to begin without that synchronisation which historians generations

---

[1] In his studies of *The British Empire before the American Revolution*, Professor L. H. Gipson has described this war as the *Great War for the Empire*, 1754–63, waged "for nine years on three oceans".

later have often seen in them. The French and Indian War began, in fact, with de Bienville's journey into the Ohio country in 1749, if indeed the clash of the fur traders in the West had ever been peaceful, and for Washington and many Virginians it was over not at the Treaty of Paris in 1763, but by the end of 1758, when the French ceased to threaten Virginia. These struggles, though forming part of a global conflict and occasionally being seen in that light by a gifted strategist like Pitt, were still largely fought for local objectives and by local time-tables. And since in times of nominal peace in Europe the defence of each colony against local enemies devolved on the colony itself, they were fought by local militia or by local volunteers—where these could be found, paid, equipped and disciplined. When the pressure eased the tension relaxed—and the volunteers disappeared.

In 1749 and 1750 tension on the Franco-British border in America was not relaxing, despite the treaty of 1748. No one was at all sure where the border was, least of all in the Ohio country. The British settlers were afraid of being pinned to the coast, and those in the West, for varied motives—security from French and Indians, land speculation or devotion to their farms—looked with alarm at French manœuvres. The French were as much the victims as the masters of their geopolitical situation. They had been less enterprising as colonisers than the British, but they had been intrepid as explorers and missionaries; in the wake of Champlain and Frontenac, La Salle and Cadillac, the outposts of New France extended from Nova Scotia westwards along the St. Lawrence to the Great Lakes, and south along the Ohio, the Illinois and the Mississippi rivers to Louisiana, named (1682) in honour of the Grand Monarch.

On the map their string of forts looked impressive and frightening, but the French were few. Furs were their chief form of marketable wealth, and though the fur trade stimulated conquest, it discouraged agriculture and kept the population scattered. They had cultivated the Indians to win the furs, and it was the Ohio Company's interest in this trade that seriously alarmed them. A French expedition, led by Céloron de Bienville, in 1749 found a number of British pioneers and traders in what it regarded as French terrritory, and ordered them to leave. Governor Dinwiddie retaliated in 1753 by sending William Trent, the "One-eyed Major", an experienced frontiersman and Indian trader, into the West to warn French squatters off British land. But on reaching Logstown, twelve miles north-west of the forks of the Ohio, Trent learned that French troops had attacked and defeated the pro-British Miami Indians, and hurriedly withdrew. In the same year the French and their barbaric forest allies built a log fort at Presquîle (now the town of Erie), and cut a road south to French Creek at the northern head of Ohio navigation. There they built Fort Le Bœuf (now Waterford, Pennsylvania). In instructions from the President of the Board of Trade, the Earl of Holderness, British colonial governors were encouraged to resist this advance and to warn the French of their encroachment on British territory. At this juncture (October 1753), Washington volunteered to carry an ultimatum on Dinwiddie's behalf to the French commander, and *en route* to judge French military strength and to prospect for good sites for possible settlement by the Ohio Company.

It was some five hundred miles to Washington's ultimate destination, Fort Le Bœuf, and it was eleven weeks before he returned with his report. He took with him a Dutchman, Van Braam, as interpreter, and Christopher Gist, an experienced scout and surveyor for the Ohio Company, whose own journal of the expedition reveals him as a man of education and quality, more skilful than Washington in the ways of Indians. It was difficult country to cross, and still is, this mountainous area of the Devil's Backbone and the Great Cacapon Forest. A gloomy British soldier on Braddock's expedition in 1755 described it as "a desolate country uninhabited by anything but wild Indians, bears and rattlesnakes". Washington reached the Forks of the Ohio, and thought it "extremely well situated for a Fort, as it has the absolute Command of both Rivers". He met sachems (chiefs) of the Delaware and Seneca Indians, and persuaded Half-King of the Senecas, a vassal of the Iroquois, to accompany him to Fort Le Bœuf.

Washington found himself acting not only as messenger but as diplomat; the French, at the outpost they had captured at Venango (now Franklin, Pennsylvania) and again a hundred miles farther on at Fort Le Bœuf, sought, with guns and rum, to detach Half-King from the British. Washington had only his own firmness as a counter-offensive. It was not sufficient and it was sorely tried. In the twilight zone between the British and French areas the Indians fought for self-preservation with procrastination and guile, and they were not an easy people for straightforward characters to understand. Indian diplomacy called for a patience Washington, at twenty-one, did not yet possess and a subtlety which never was his *forte*. Instructed to deal with the French, his journal suggests that he thought of the Indians largely as complicating the issue, whereas to Joincaré, the half-Seneca commander at Venango, and his superiors, they were part of the stakes for which they fought.

The French treated Washington with the courtesy, and indeed with the frankness, of gentlemanly adversaries :

"The Wine, as they dosed themselves pretty plentifully with it, soon banished the Restraint. . . . They told me, That it was their Absolute Design to take Possession of the Ohio, and by G— they would do it; for that altho' they were sensible the English could raise two men for their one, yet they know their Motions were too slow and dilatory to prevent any undertaking of theirs. They pretend to have an undoubted Right to the River from a Discovery made by one La Salle 60 years ago."

At Fort Le Bœuf, Washington obtained a reply to Dinwiddie's letter, which amounted to a polite refusal by the French to pay any attention to the Governor's orders. He kept his eyes open while he waited, and, impatient to convey his resultant alarm, he found the diplomatic dalliance of French and Indians hard to endure. He finally returned, in bitter weather, by canoe down French Creek and overland from Venango. The horses were too weak to carry packs, and against Gist's advice Washington and his guide pushed ahead on foot. They were fired upon by a French Indian—a poor shot. They crossed a deep ice-choked river by an improvised raft, from which Washington fell; he spent the night in a soaked jacket on an island in the river with the water itself freezing. "The Cold was so extremely severe, that Mr. Gist had all his Fingers, and Some of his Toes frozen"; but Washington, incredibly, suffered no ill-effects.

If not a story of unqualified diplomatic skill, it is a saga of physical endurance and great tenacity of will.

The journey was not the end of Washington's difficulties. On reporting to Dinwiddie, in January 1754, the Governor asked him to put his notes into connected form to be laid before the legislature next day. He worked through the night on the account, to which he prefixed a characteristic apology because he had "no leisure to consult of a new and proper Form to offer it in, or to correct or amend the Diction". It was published both in Virginia and in England, and the extant copies of it are to-day among the rarest of American incunabula. *The Journal of Major George Washington* made it clear that a frontier conflict was imminent and was used to headline the war-guilt of the French. The Virginia Assembly testified its "approbation of his proceedings" by voting him the sum of £50.

It was not enough, however, to awaken Britain to the menace, for it would take time for the Home Government to act. The French meantime must be forestalled, and there must be sent to the Forks a covering force to protect the party under Trent already on its way to build the Company's fort. Other colonies must be asked to share the burden. But from the other colonies there was scant support for what might appear as Virginian land-grabbing, and even the Virginian Burgesses were hesitant. They did, however, vote Dinwiddie £10,000 and authority to raise six companies, even if they hedged the grant about with an embarrassing committee of nine to act as a check on the Governor, to his evident displeasure—"monstrously unconstitutional", "a republican way of thinking". Washington, who five days after his return had been charged with the task of calling out and training his militia in the Northern Neck, was quickly diverted into the task of enlisting and training the volunteers that this new grant made possible, and who could be moved at will, as the militia could not. These volunteers Washington called "loose, idle persons that are quite destitute of House and Home; and I may truely say, many of them of Cloaths". Though Washington's language, then and later, about his troops lacks the pungency of Wellington's, it clearly reflects similar sentiments, as in

24

the end it reflects a similar pride in what such recruits would dare and endure.

In April 1754, as Lieutenant-Colonel and second-in-command to Colonel Joshua Fry, who was to follow with the main force, Washington set off again for the Ohio. His problems seemed endless. No uniforms and no credit with which to buy them; utterly inadequate drill and discipline, largely because of a lack of N.C.O.s; slowness of recruitment; lack of provisions and supplies; difficult relations between militia and volunteers, and between British regulars, if and when they arrived, and local recruits; differences of pay between regular and locally recruited officers—a difference of 10s. per day, as Washington promptly noted; the constant threat of desertion. His Colonel, Joshua Fry, English-born and Oxford-educated, a Professor of Mathematics at William and Mary College at Williamsburg, died in the Valley without ever reaching his forward troops. There was no one who knew how long it would take two hundred raw recruits to march to the Forks and how many wagons and horses would be needed to transport and provision them and supply their ammunition; there were no drill-sergeants in either the European or the Indian versions of war. It was in overcoming these difficulties, in 1754 as in 1776, that Washington built his military reputation.

When he reached Wills Creek, a messenger met him with the news that his effort was all in vain : the fort at the Forks was in French hands, and it was named after their commander, Du Quesne. This was but the beginning of Washington's misfortunes. It is true that three more companies of the Virginia Regiment reached him, and an Independent Company from South Carolina under Captain Mackay. But the Independent Company, as part of the British establishment in the colonies, was commanded by regular officers with a King's, as distinct from a Governor's, commission, and enjoyed higher pay and a certain sense of superiority. This made for difficulty rather than for strength : was Washington as a colonial Colonel inferior to a regular Captain? All Dinwiddie could do by way of decision was to plead that he should not allow "some punctillios about command" to interfere with the expedition; but he was, and remained, fastidious about his rank and dignity.

Though all the evidence pointed to an imminent French advance in strength—confirmed by the steady disappearances of the few friendly Indians, who could smell the way the winds blew in the forest with uncanny accuracy—Washington moved slowly forward, four miles a day at best along a trail his men tried to widen into a road. His small force cast around for information and got baffling rumours. Hearing from friendly Indians of a party of French soldiers near by, they surrounded them (May 1754) and attacked them without warning, killing ten, including the leader, Jumonville, and capturing twenty-one; the rest were wounded and fell victim to the Indians, who, Washington reported, "bereiv'd them of their scalps". Unhappily the prisoners claimed that they were on a mission like his own the year before, and on Jumonville's body there was found a *sommation* addressed to the commander of the English troops on the lands of the King of France, ordering him to leave. This did not worry Washington; the men were spies; having seized the fort, there could be no further claims of diplomatic immunity; the line between a summons to withdraw carried by an armed party of thirty men and a reconnoitre in strength was now, he argued, hard to draw. The French took up the challenge.

Encouraged by this success, Washington moved forward to Gist's (the trader's) settlement, taking his puny but valuable nine swivel guns with him; then, at reports of French advances, he hurriedly fell back to an improvised fort at Great Meadows, aptly named Fort Necessity, badly sited in an open, swampy hollow over which a near-by hill gave a commanding view. Here (3rd July 1754) some four hundred hungry and ill-equipped men were attacked by an infinitely superior French force under Jumonville's brother, with Indians, trees, ammunition and skill as their allies; after a nine-hour siege of blinding rain and accurate fire, Washington's force was compelled to surrender. The end was grim, for, though food was scarce, rum was plentiful and many of his men were drunk. There were thirty dead, seventy wounded and more dropped out or deserted on the long, humiliating haul back to the Valley. The surrender terms included an acknowledgment that the attack on Jumonville was an assassination". Washington and his colleagues claimed that, as translated by Van Braam, by the light of a guttering candle, in a rainstorm that made the soggy document hard to decipher, he was not aware that he was admitting to such a description. This document, however, along with Washington's journal and drafts of letters, captured in Fort Necessity, was published in France "strangely metamorphosed," as Washington put it, and served to visit the war guilt on Virginia.

In some ways Washington's eagerness to attack the Jumonville party was the cause of the Seven Years War : "a trifling action, but remarkable for giving date to the War", as Horace Walpole described it. His letters and notes, however distorted by the French, suggest a commander brash and proud, untrained as yet in frontier warfare. Yet the unquestioning courage, the sheer persistence, the unyielding vitality and endurance, have their own quality. The campaign of 1754, was so ineptly managed, from Williamsburg and London as well as in the Alleghenies, that only a man of singular courage and singular lack of imagination could have carried on at all. Some critical contemporary judgments were made. William Johnson, one of the wisest of Britain's Indian administrators, thought Washington lacking in "prudence and circumspection". "I doubt his being too ambitious of acquiring all the honour or as much as he could before the rest joined him." Half-King thought him good-natured but inexperienced and indifferent to the advice of the Indians. Governor Sharpe of Maryland, who had sent no reinforcements, spoke of his "unmilitary conduct". Young Washington was learning the hard and solitary way : how not to treat Indians and French, how not and where not to site forts, how not to get on with colleagues. He was learning the lessons in a colony still apathetic about the French threat. Dinwiddie drew this sustenance from the disaster—until it occurred "not three men would believe a syllable of the danger that threatened them", but under its impact he found a slow change of heart both in Williamsburg and in London : the Assembly voted him £20,000, the Home Government sent him £10,000 in specie with the promise of ten thousand more, and two thousand firearms.

Between Washington and Dinwiddie, however, relations cooled. After his return to Williamsburg, the Governor had rashly ordered him back to attempt to destroy the French communications and corn, which Washington correctly said was impossible in the condition of his men. Dinwiddie refused to return French prisoners as Washington had undertaken to have done in the terms of his capitulation. The Governor even proposed to solve the question of the standing of royal as against colonial officers by breaking up the Virginia Regiment into separate companies and appointing no colonial to a higher rank than captain, a sharp blow to Washington's pride. The outcome was his resignation from the service, October 1754. For a month or two he was a civilian again, at Fredericksburg and Mount Vernon. The interlude was brief. In March, 1755, Edward Braddock with two under-strength regiments of British troops landed at Alexandria.

On arrival in Virginia, Major-General Edward Braddock had already seen forty-five years of army service. Blunt and peppery in manner, a rigorous martinet and scornful of the colonists, he had been thoroughly trained in the formal rules of eighteenth-century warfare as understood in Europe. He appointed Washington, probably on Dinwiddie's recommendation, to his military "family" as a volunteer aide, which avoided the matter of rank, and which gave him the chance to act as the eyes and ears of the General, whom he came to esteem highly. Braddock brought a new efficiency to the campaign, able aides and impressive artillery. By the end of May 1755 there were some twenty-two hundred men assembled at Fort Cumberland.

These appearances proved deceptive, and Braddock had from the beginning no joy in the expedition. The difficulties that had faced Washington recurred on an even vaster scale. Only Benjamin Franklin fulfilled his contracts to supply pack-animals and wagons. The Quartermaster-General, Sir John St. Clair, "stormed like a lion rampant", but to little avail. Washington endorsed his Generals' strictures on colonial, in this case Pennsylvanian, apathy—"You may with almost equal success attempt to raise the dead . . . as the force of this Country." Braddock and his staff were themselves culpable in miscalculating distances and underestimating difficulties. Wagons were lost and artillery moved with despairing slowness, sometimes only two miles a day. On

16th June Washington proposed that the General should push ahead with a chosen detachment, and let the wagons follow more slowly, lest the French reinforce Fort Du Quesne before the British reach it. The plan was adopted, and a column of thirteen hundred men, with howitzers and twelve-pounders, began to make speedier progress towards the Monongahela, cutting a twelve-foot-wide path through the forest. Even so, it was not until the 7th July that they neared the mouth of Turtle Creek, which entered the Monongahela about ten miles south-east of the fort.

"The music, the banners, the mounted officers, the troop of light cavalry, the naval detachment, the red-coated regulars, the blue-coated Virginians, the wagons and tumbrils, cannon, howitzers and coe-horns [light grenade-throwing mortars], the train of pack horses, and the droves of cattle, passed in long procession through the rippling shallows, and slowly entered the bordering forest."

Such is Parkman's description of the crossing on the 8th. And Washington, not yet recovered from an attack of dysentery, or "bloody flux", insisted on riding forward to join Braddock and to enjoy the spectacle. The French sent forward to oppose them a force of some nine hundred, of whom over six hundred were Indians, with a gallant French leader, Beaujeu, in the war-paint of an Indian brave. The engagement was short, unplanned but dramatic. Braddock was not taken by surprise, but he took fewer precautions once he had made the dangerous double crossing of the river. His column was in so narrow a path that it could not manœuvre. It was surrounded by the Indians, who poured fire into it from behind the trees; a charge into the forest arranged with a precision learnt on the fields of Flanders and bravely attempted, proved disastrous, and when amid the smoke and the uncanny, echoing war-whoops the scalping knife was seen panic began. The regulars "broke and ran", said Washington, "as sheep pursued by dogs". Even so they had stood their ground as a huddled target for over two hours. And Washington exempted the Virginians from criticism—they "behav'd like Men and died like Soldiers". Braddock was killed, muttering his praise of the Virginian "blues", and with his last breath saying of the French, "We shall better know how to deal with them another time". Of his eighty-six officers, sixty-three were killed or wounded. Washington, behaving on that day with pre-eminent courage, had two horses killed under him and his clothes torn by four bullets. Despite his condition, he had at Braddock's order ridden back to warn Dunbar, with the rear party, and to request help. But Dunbar, commanding on the death of Braddock, destroyed his wagons and guns, to Washington's horror, and proceeded to put what space he could between himself and the French. He made for Philadelphia, and went into winter quarters there in the middle of August, taking Virginian troops with him. "The whole conduct of Colonel Dunbar", wrote Dinwiddie, "appears to me monstrous."

The French were in no eagerness to pursue. They had tried an attack as a last resort against apparently overwhelming odds. They owed their victory as much to the war-whoops and accurate fire of their savage allies as to any skill of their own. The field was left to Indian pillage and murder : those prisoners brought into the French fort were burnt at the stake by the Delawares and Mingoes, and news of the disaster and of its consequences sent another tremor of fear along the Allegheny frontier. The British plan had included attempts by Governor Shirley of Massachusetts to capture Niagara and by Sir William Johnson to take Crown Point, and these failed also. The only success—the seizure of Acadia by volunteers from New England—was marred by the forcible removal of the French from their homes, an act of unnecessary cruelty.

In August 1755, Washington was appointed Colonel and Commander-in-Chief of all Virginia's forces. He had his customary doubts about accepting the command—"but the solicitations of the country overcame my objections". His task, indeed, was thankless. Indian savagery was now unleashed against the frontier counties, sudden and erratic attacks occurring at least monthly along three hundred miles. Settlers, stricken by rumour and panic, fled eastwards. The militia, last line of defence, was timid, untrained and ill-equipped. On paper Washington was empowered to recruit twelve hundred men into the Virginia Regiment, but his force was never more than nine hundred, sometimes only three hundred, and his recruits often paupers and criminals. His reserve supply of muskets had gone north for the operations against Niagara and Crown Point. His powers of discipline were limited by the militia law of August 1755, and even some of his officers, on detached duty, became slack and drunken. Chief of his problems, however, was the claim of Captain Dagworthy, stationed at Fort Cumberland with only thirty Marylanders and no regulars, to be the holder of a King's commission, and therefore to take precedence over colonial officers in command at the fort.

This dispute over seniority was submitted to Governor Shirley of Massachusetts, the acting British commander in North America, who replied evasively. Washington thereupon won Dinwiddie's approval for a personal appeal to Shirley, and in February and March 1756, undertook the five-hundred-mile journey to Boston, the longest he had made.

On 1st March, the *Boston Gazette* announced the arrival of "the Hon. Col. Washington, a gentleman who has deservedly a high reputation for military skill and valor, though success has not always attended his undertakings". Shirley now decided that Dagworthy ranked only as a provincial captain "where there are no troops joined", but Washington's satisfaction was modified by the news that, just before his arrival in Boston, Shirley had appointed Governor Sharpe of Maryland to head all the troops to be raised in Pennsylvania, Maryland, Virginia and South Carolina for the next Du Quesne expedition.

On 30th March, Washington was back in Williamsburg. His long and leisurely journey had given him some knowledge of the northern colonies, of the cities of Philadelphia, Boston and New York; it brought personal contact with the admired Shirley, and with Sharpe; and it led him to reflect on his prospects. He was alarmed by Shirley's revelation of a projected campaign against Niagara—Virginia would again be left to her fate. If he had triumphed over Dagworthy, he had now to placate Sharpe. He rode home "fully resolved to resign my commission", but Speaker Robinson's persuasions and new Indian threats drove away his gloom. He determined instead to ask Sharpe's approval for the place of second officer in the next offensive against Du Quesne.

Plans for this attack hung fire, and in 1756 and 1757 Virginia's role was defensive. Washington strove to bring the regiment to full strength and to have the militia law improved. He recommended his officers to study Humphrey Bland's *Treatise of Military Discipline,* the classic military manual of the day. By the summer of 1756 and with Dinwiddie's tacit support, Washington was becoming stern. He insisted that a deserter and a sergeant who had shown cowardice, and who had been condemned by court-martial, be put to death before the eyes of the newly drafted men. Swearing was made punishable by twenty-five lashes, drunkenness with fifty. "Discipline", said Washington, "is the soul of an army." On 15th August his authority was enhanced : the official declaration of war by Britain against France, proclaimed 17th May at home, was read to his three companies in his headquarters at Winchester with "great parade". Cannon were thrice discharged and three rounds of musketry were fired. The drums they tapped were four old ones, in broken condition.

He strove, too, to build a number of small forts to secure the frontiers, and from which venturesome spirits might lead occasional expeditions against the Indians, as Andrew Lewis did against the Shawnee towns. By inclination, Washington favoured the expeditions rather than the forts, but the Assembly, "the chimney-corner politicians", insisted on defence. By the end of 1756, twenty-seven forts or stockades dotted the Allegheny frontier from Fort Cumberland to the North Carolina line. In October 1756, Washington toured the frontier, travelling farther south than he had ever been before. Like Dinwiddie, he had from the beginning seen the need for support from the Indians—their absence had wrecked his own earlier ventures. "Indians are the only match for Indians, and without these we shall ever fight upon unequal terms." A "Scalp Market" was established, in which quotation on the scalps of hostile Indians ranged from £10 in 1755 to £45 in 1758. But it was an uphill task : the management of Indian affairs was taken from him; responsibility for Fort Cumberland was transferred to Maryland; his troops, unclothed, unfed, unpaid, were still too few to be anything but "a breakfast to the French and their Indians"; the Burgesses were frankly unwilling to draft anyone who had a vote.

In November 1757, Washington took ill with dysentery

and was away from duty for five months. The prospect was as bleak elsewhere. In July Lord Loudoun, the new commander in North America, had had to abandon the proposed attack on Louisburg. In August the French under Montcalm had attacked and destroyed Fort William Henry at the lower end of Lake George, and what was left of its garrison had been murdered by the Indians.

When Washington returned to duty in April 1758, the situation had changed. Pitt, recalled as Secretary of State in June 1757, had planned a three-fold attack, on not unfamiliar lines, but with new and young commanders, with newly raised regiments, not least those from the Scottish Highlands, and with close and effective support from the Navy. Amherst, with thirty-year-old Wolfe as one of his brigadiers, was to lead a new expedition against Louisburg as a preliminary to an attack on Quebec; Abercromby was to advance on Ticonderoga; Brigadier-General John Forbes of the 17th Foot was to take the much-contested road for Fort Du Quesne. Virginia was to have two regiments, the second to be commanded by twenty-nine-year-old William Byrd III, and they were to be employed in the common cause. At last one of Washington's problems was settled : American officers would in future take rank with the regulars, according to the date of their commissions.

Forbes' campaign makes happier reading than Braddock's. Though the road was almost as difficult, he chose a new route, from Raystown, the present Bedford, Pennsylvania, to Loyal Hannon, and he established depots as he advanced. Washington fought the decision to go through Pennsylvania with a Virginian patriotism and a soldierly lack of discretion which almost lost him Forbes' goodwill. Forbes had three times as many troops as Braddock : 7,000 men, of whom about 1,400 were Highlanders. When, in July 1758, Washington and Byrd led their regiments into Raystown, they were almost at full strength, and were, in St. Clair's opinion, "a fine body of men". This contrast with 1755 reflected not only the bounty offered them and the short period of enlistment (to December 1758) but the years of training at Washington's hands. He was complimented not only on the speed of his advance from Fort Cumberland but on the utility of his men's dress. Hunting shirts and leggings became the fashion.

Washington's dejection over the choice of route was increased by the slow progress of the main expedition. Forbes' own dilatory tactics, however, masked manœuvres to win the Indians from the French. They were risky, since the weather was rapidly worsening and, under the terms of its enlistment, the Second Virginia Regiment would cease to exist on the 1st January; but they were successful. On 27th October, a treaty was signed with the Indians, and reports came of a French withdrawal. Forbes thereupon ordered three lightly-equipped brigades to drive on the fort, to the third of which he appointed Washington, and he himself, a dying man, travelled in a litter at their head. On 16th November, Washington's troops began cutting the last road to Du Quesne. Nine days later they reached it, and found a smoking, deserted ruin. In the north, the capture of Fort Frontenac on Lake Ontario by Bradstreet, a colonel of militia from Maine, had cut the link between Canada and the Ohio. After five years of frontier violence, peace returned to Virgina's Valley and its farms. Before the year was out, Brigadier Washington rode back to the Tidewater exhausted but content. He resigned his commission on 31st December.

Chapter Three

Planter and Burgess: Virginia
(1759—1774)

WASHINGTON reached Williamsburg on 30th December 1758, and on 6th January 1759 he married Martha Dandridge Custis, pretty and plump and by repute the wealthiest widow in Virginia. There are several traditional but unreliable tales of their first meeting. All that is certain is that Washington visited the Custis' White House on the Pamunkey, fifteen miles from Williamsburg, in March 1758, when he was recovering from his illness. In his ledger against 4th May 1758 is an entry for the purchase of a ring. Few of Washington's letters to his wife have survived, but there does remain one, laconic and uncharacteristic, dated 20th July 1758, "to one whose life is now inseparable from mine" and signed by "your ever faithful and affectionate friend", which, if it is genuine, at least confirms that by July they were engaged.

What is more puzzling is that on 12th September Washington appears to have written a more characteristic and involved letter to Sally Fairfax, which can only be read as a declaration of his love for her, the wife of his best friend.

"You have drawn me, dear Madame, or rather I have drawn myself, into an honest confession of a simple Fact. Misconstrue not my meaning; doubt it not, nor expose it. The world has no business to know the object of my Love, declared in this manner to you, when I want to conceal it."

This letter was printed entire in the *New York Herald,* 30th March 1877, in an account of a collection of autographs to be sold at auction the following day. It was duly sold, but no record of the purchaser was kept, and the letter has completely disappeared. Its authenticity is thus open to question. Sally Fairfax's reply has also disappeared, but Washington's letter of the 25th begins :

"Dear Madam : Do we still misunderstand the true meaning of each other's letters? I think it must appear so, tho' I would feign hope the contrary, as I cannot speak plainer without—but I'll say no more and leave you to guess the rest."

This is tenuous evidence, but upon this, as upon his verses to a "Lowland Beauty" and his meeting with Mary Philipse during his four-day stay in New York in 1756, the "love life" of Washington has been precariously built. Romantic biographers have made what they can out of the slender material; cynics have—reluctantly—praised his self-control and "discretion"; admirers have acclaimed his standards, and correctly so. For Washington, if not romantic, was at least bewilderingly frank. If the letter of 12th September is genuine, it is evidence that before his marriage and before going into action with Forbes he wanted Sally Fairfax to know of his love for her; equally, he wanted her to know that "there is a Destiny which has the sovereign control of our actions not to be resisted by the strongest efforts of Human Nature". Forty years later, when Belvoir was a gutted ruin and Sally a widow living in England, Washington wrote to her that he still looked back on his days in her company as the happiest in his life. He found in Martha "an agreable Consort", as he put it, but he never forgot Sally.

In January 1759, then, Washington added to his own 5,000 acres and 49 slaves the wealth of the Custis plantation, 17,000 acres, a fortune set at £23,000, some 300 slaves and a town house in the colonial capital at Williamsburg. The wealth brought the responsibilities of trusteeship, for two-thirds of the estate were to pass, when they came of age, to his wife's two children, John Parke Custis ("Jacky"), aged four, and Martha Parke Custis ("Patsy"), aged two. To these children his wife was devoted : Jacky was spoilt by his mother's indulgence, and his education—or rather his un-willingness to suffer it—became a sore perplexity to his step-father; Patsy was a delicate child whose death from epilepsy at seventeen was a sad blow, for there were no children of Washington's own.

The fifteen years that followed the marriage were years of activity and contentment—and, as a result, lean years in the Washington records. Letters pleading for supplies and money, and threats of resignation, are replaced by letters to

Robert Cary, his London agent, expressing concern over tobacco sales and containing invoices for goods—busts of soldiers for the drawing-room, a ruffled negligee of salmon-coloured taffeta, "fashionable dressed" dolls, reflecting his new and elegant domesticity. The so-called *Diaries* are not the records of an inner life, but business jottings, notes on the state of the crops, methodical accounts of experiments with plants and seed and fertiliser, assessments of the merits of tenants and slaves and brood mares. Yet these years are important, not only for the evidence of patient administration of estates, or of the increasing demands on Washington as justice, vestryman, burgess and good neighbour, but as evidence, too, of the methodical habits, the managerial capacity, the concern for detail, that were later to be of such value in the conduct of the war.

When Washington took up residence at Mount Vernon he assumed duties as extensive as those of any field-officer in war. Control over the Custis plantations on the York he left largely to an efficient overseer, Joseph Valentine, but on his own farms he exercised a direct responsibility. The Mount Vernon estate covered 4,000 acres, divided into five farms, each with an overseer's house, barns and stables, and quarters for slaves. Slaves and white tenants alike were, in general, ignorant and shiftless, and needed firm and prudent handling. Nor was Washington experienced as a plantation owner and scientific farmer; though all his early life was spent on farms and among horses, he was by choice and training a surveyor and a woodsman. To his new responsibility he brought his customary thoroughness. He sent for books from London—"The newest, and most approv'd Treatise of Agriculture—besides this, send me a small piece in Octavo—call'd a New System of Agriculture, or a Speedy Way to Grow Rich." He sent for agricultural implements and tried to devise his own—"Spent the greatest part of the day in making a plow of my own Invention."

Tobacco was the staple crop, and Washington sought to grow the finest in the valley of the Potomac. It was not an easy task, for every planter in Virginia cultivated it, and judging both the plant and the weather at the several critical stages of growing, curing and packing was a matter of great skill, from planning the work of the slaves and clearing new land to the delivery of the hogsheads at the inspection ware-houses near the fall-line, where they were checked by officials selected by the justices. The receipts issued by these inspectors, the tobacco-notes, were the paper money of the colony. Most of the hogsheads were consigned after inspection directly to the ships bound for Britain, which had a monopoly of the trade. A fleet of about a hundred and twenty vessels went annually to Chesapeake Bay and moved on the average 90,000 hogsheads (each about 1,000 lb.) from Virginia and Maryland. The planter had then to watch the prices his tobacco brought on the British market, and against his tobacco credits order the farm equipment and tools, hard-ware and textiles, the luxuries and the necessities, not for a family only but for a community often the size of a village.

Washington was business-like, and he was generous, especially to comrades of the war and to friends and neigh-bours, for many of whom he was banker, creditor and coun-sellor. But he soon discovered at first hand how perilous the tobacco economy was. He found himself, in 1761, £2,000 in debt to his London agents, and, with all his planning and industry, he failed to obtain the price for his Potomac to-bacco that he needed. Almost all the planters were in debt to each other and to London, and the main reason was their obsession with a single crop. They had produced it for a century and a half, and had on its profits lived comfortable, some of them ostentatious, lives. But the crop was destruc-tive of the land, and depended on a slave labour force which was, to judge it by economic standards alone, unenterprising and expensive; there was a chronic shortage of specie and an adverse exchange. Tobacco-notes were the only currency until the French and Indian War drove the colony to the printing-press, with the usual results. Britain sent manu-factured goods, not coin, in exchange for tobacco; what coins did circulate were foreign and often clipped—doubloons, Spanish pistoles and pieces of eight, German ducats and French guineas and Portuguese moidores, exchanged for the pitch and tar, turpentine and beef the colony sent to the West Indian islands. If the tobacco was consigned to London, local factors, freight and insurance charges, export taxes, the duties to be paid in Britain and the London or Glasgow merchants' commission, the conspiracy, as it seemed in Virginia, of British merchants to keep down the prices they offered, and the pilfering *en route*—these might eat up 80 per cent. or more of what the crop brought. Little wonder that in Jefferson's view the Virginian planters were "a species of property annexed to certain mercantile houses in London". He estimated that Virginians owed at least £2,000,000 sterling to British creditors on the eve of the Revolution—twenty-five times the total amount of currency in the colony.

Washington was both more fortunate and more enterprising than his fellows; he had a greater degree of security than most from the wealth of the Custis plantations, which were more productive than his own, and he had the wit to see that tobacco was no longer a reliable source of wealth to Virginia. By 1763 he was beginning to experiment; by 1768 he had ceased to grow tobacco on his Potomac farms, and wheat had become the main crop; by 1770 he was planning a new and larger mill to grind his own, and his neighbours', wheat into flour. This meant not only self-sufficiency as a farmer but independence of the British market. By 1769 fishing on the Potomac was sufficient to allow a small shipment to Antigua. By 1772 Washington was shipping 270 barrels of flour to the West Indies, too; rather "musty" flour, he confessed, but it would permit the buying of slaves, if "choice ones" could be got for less than £40 a head.

This shift from tobacco to wheat was successful, and the earnings went into a steady stream of acres held and slaves owned. The change reduced the need for field hands, but there was land to be bought up—of those who failed to read the signs and went under, and land, too, in the West, if it could be reached and surveyed and patented. By 1770 Washington owned over 9,000 acres, in six different counties. Martha for her part was superintendent of a large manufacturing establishment, staffed by negro labour. In one year she wove 815 yards of linen, 365 yards of wool, 144 yards of linsey, 40 yards of cotton. She produced patterned material, too—striped cotton, striped and plaided woollens, dimity, broadcloth, draper, fustian and ticking for beds. She ran a dairy and a smoke-house, and managed a home that now, as later, was more like a large hotel.

Success as a planter brought responsibilities. Washington was a trustee of the town of Alexandria. He became vestryman and warden of Truro Parish, and in September 1768 a Justice of the County Court of Fairfax, a body which was not only judicial but legislative and electoral, too. The court tried civil and criminal cases, appointed county officers, supervised elections, roads, bridges, ferries, ordinaries or inns, and performed the thousand and one functions of local government. To be vestryman, justice and burgess was the mark of the successful gentleman, for the same people served in all three capacities, a self-perpetuating aristocracy of talent.

Planters in eighteenth-century Virginia dominated the government as well as the economy. They not only outnumbered lawyers, lawyers were normally planters as well. Since land was cheap, society was fluid; for the same reason prestige lay with those "long-tailed" families with extensive acres and many slaves, living, normally, in the Tidewater, and building the Georgian mansions that still grace the James River. The operation of a plantation was a most public activity, and success in it was as efficient a method of indicating capacity for public service as any of the more democratic devices of later centuries. It was from the planter class that the twelve members of the Council were chosen, and the same class provided most of the hundred and four members of the House of Burgesses (two members for each County, one for the College of William and Mary, and one each for Jamestown, Williamsburg and Norfolk). Every free adult male possessing twenty-five acres of land with a house or plantation, or one hundred acres of unsettled land, had the suffrage. Elections were public and lively, voting oral, and "refreshments"—of rum punch—abundant. It was the practice "to go merry to the Court House".

From 1758 to 1765 Washington was Burgess for Frederick County, from 1765 for Fairfax. At least once a year, more often twice or thrice, he visited Williamsburg and met the Governor, the Council and his fellow Burgesses. The "public times" in the leafy small town, with its elegantly proportioned brick Capitol, Governor's Palace and College, were exciting, socially and politically, and increasingly so after 1765. But Washington was not prominent in debate : words did not come easily to him either in speech or in writing. He was not constant in attendance : unlike Jefferson, he has left no record of seeing Patrick Henry when the parson's cause was raised ("He seemed to me to speak as Homer wrote," said Jefferson), or of staying to hear the Stamp Act Resolves introduced in 1765. It took him at least three days' hard riding, and longer if he travelled with Martha in his green and gilt coach, to reach Williamsburg from the Northern Neck, and with interests in Frederick and on the York, the increasing calls to the capital could not always be heeded. From the beginning, however, he was a member of one of the most important committees, that on Propositions and Grievances. And he took up one cause particularly, on their behalf as on his own. The Virginia soldiers of 1754 had been promised 200,000 acres of bounty land on the Ohio, land which needed to be secured and surveyed and divided up equitably among them. By a royal proclamation of 1763, further offers of land to ex-soldiers had been made, if they chose to apply for it. For ten years Washington pressed the justice and the urgency of these claims on the Governor and the Assembly, and through them on the British Government in London.

This land problem was not unlike that facing his first hero, Lord Fairfax, in 1745. There was the same dispute as before over colonial boundaries, over Virginia's sea-to-sea claims and the counter-claims of her neighbours, especially Pennsylvania, with her wily Benjamin Franklin at work in London; and the attitude of the Home Government was just as hesitant. The Proclamation Line of 1763 had forbidden colonial settlement west of the Allegheny watershed; in the same year, the Indian rising, miscalled the Conspiracy of Pontiac, alarmed the Home Government, and two years were to pass before it was suppressed; more garrisons were needed and various new colonies like "Vandalia" were planned athwart the line of Virginia's—and Washington's—ambitions. Writing to an old friend of the Forbes' expedition, William Crawford, living on the Youghiogheny, in 1767, Washington confided that he had never seen the Proclamation except as "a temporary expedient to quiet the minds of the Indians". Crawford agreed to act as Washington's land agent and surveyor in the west, but discretion was the order of the day. "I might be censured for the opinion I have given in respect to the King's proclamation." Washington recommended "silent management . . . snugly carried on by you under the pretence of hunting other game".

By 1768 Washington's foresight was rewarded and the need for silence in management less imperative. The Treaty of Fort Stanwix with the Iroquois and the Treaty of Hard Labour with the Cherokees drew a new line and pushed the area of potential settlement farther west. In 1769 the Governor and Council agreed that the promise to the volunteers of 1754 should be honoured. As Washington knew the men, they were to make their claims to him and he was to certify them as valid. Further assurance came in 1770 by the Treaty of Lochaber with the Cherokees. In August 1770, he met claimants at Fredericksburg. On 5th October, with his friend and war-time surgeon, James Craik, and three servants, he set off on his fifth journey to the Ohio, to see the land for himself. By 1771 the entitlement of bounty land was worked out for each man—as a field-officer Washington was to get 15,000 acres plus some share of the extra acres for those who had borne the expense of the surveys. In the end he secured some 24,000 acres, since he bought up the claims of many who were too poor to help finance the work or who were sceptical of the final outcome. And by his own visit to the Ohio and the Great Kanawha, and by his canniness in exhorting Crawford to act on his behalf, he had acquired acres that were as rich as they were extensive. He had obviously been well rewarded. Yet the fact remains that under any system of distribution according to rank, Washington merited his share, and that without his persistence in petitioning the Governor, in organising the claimants and in visiting the Ohio, it is possible that the promise of 1754 would have been unredeemed.

If Washington's growing patience and steady industry are the most striking features of these years, more significant is the unquestioning faith in land, especially in western land, and in its future. His advice to Captain Posey is characteristic: ". . . look to Frederick, and see what fortunes were made by the Hites and first takers up of those lands : Nay, how the greatest estates we have in this Colony were made. Was it not by taking up and purchasing at very low rates the rich black lands which were thought nothing of in those days, but are now the most valuable lands that we possess?"

He subscribed to a new and ambitious Mississippi Company, which sent an agent to Britain to solicit a grant of land sufficient to allow each member of the company 50,000 acres on the Mississippi River, an enterprise that came to nought. In 1763 Washington and some of his planter friends undertook to drain and reclaim what they could of the Great Dismal Swamp, on the Virginia–North Carolina line. He was interested in West Florida; when the young James Wood, son of his old political sponsor in Frederick County, visited that area, he was instructed to keep his eye open for land for Washington. The time would come when he would take even bigger gambles to hold what was his own in the rich river bottoms and the broad acres.

One aspect of this faith in the development of the West was a concern with possible routes of trade and traffic. As he had lost favour with Forbes because of his over-insistence on the importance of the Fort Cumberland–Potomac road to the West, so in the years from 1769 to 1773 Washington was again urging the advantages of this route over all others. In 1769 the House of Burgesses *Ordered* "that leave be given to bring in a bill for clearing and making navigable the River Potomac from the Great Falls of the said River up to Fort Cumberland and that Mr. Richard Henry Lee and Mr. Washington do prepare and bring in the same".

Under Washington's initiative, an Act was passed providing for the raising of money by subscription and by lottery, and for public tolls. "The opening of the Potomack", he argued, "will at once fix the trade of the western country at least till it may be conducted through the Mississippi, [by New Orleans] through that channel, and end in amazing advantages to these two Colonies". He feared, as in 1758, that "ill-timed parsimony and supineness" on Virginia's part would allow the initiative to pass to the Susquehanna valley and Philadelphia. Again and again in his letters he sees the opportunity for the Potomac to harness to itself the "trade of a rising empire". And if the Potomac prospered, so would the lands and farms on its creeks and runs, Mount Vernon among them. He subscribed £500 to the enterprise, but it had come to nothing on the outbreak of the revolution. When the project was again raised, it was to have even more momentous results : it was out of the discussions on the Potomac trade that the call arose for the summoning of the Convention which, in 1787, drew up the Constitution.

To the course of the debate between colony and mother country, proceeding in the east wing of the Capitol in Williamsburg, Washington paid less attention.[1] At the close of the Seven Years War, having liberated the colonies from both French and Indian threats largely by the use of regular troops, Parliament sought to meet part of the cost of the maintenance of a military garrison in America by imposing internal taxes and by tightening up existing laws. The British national debt, it was argued, had been doubled; the colonists were paying very little towards the costs of the Empire as such. This decision was a natural conclusion from war-time experiences. Dinwiddie, it will be recalled, had pressed for troops from Britain, and had even suggested in 1754 that they should be supported by a poll-tax of half a crown levied on all the colonists and paid as Parliament should direct. He prophesied that the colonists would be "inflamed if they hear of my making this Proposal, as they are averse to all Taxes". The mother country was convinced that they were lightly taxed and were living in luxury. The unseemly practice of begging colonial assemblies to pay their share of military expenses should stop. The days of "salutary neglect" were over.

The attempt by the Home Government after 1763 to enforce Acts of Trade that had been tacitly abandoned and to enact new legislation was also the result of an emergent, self-conscious sense of Empire, fostered by the successes of Pitt and his lieutenants and by the failure of the Indian policies of the individual colonies. The Indian rising of 1763–5 in the West seemed to be warning of a savage and ceaseless conflict unless Britain intervened with troops to protect the land-rights of the tribes, and followed up her intervention

---

[1] For an illuminating account of the development of revolutionary feeling in Virginia from 1765 to 1776, see Max Beloff : *Thomas Jefferson and American Democracy,* a companion volume in this series.

by creating an Indian reserve. Regulations governing the work of missionaries and the supply of firearms and fire-water for Indians were drawn up, and the powers of the two superintendents of Indian Affairs were increased. This policy was expensive and hard to enforce. The British interest was in furs, the colonial in land. The only practical result was frustration among land claimants and traders and a new frontier war in 1774.

This new imperial vigour had even sharper impact on the Tidewater, for Virginia, like the other colonies, was asked to pay part of the cost of frontier defence and of naval security. The Sugar Act of 1764 tightened up the derelict Molasses Act. The Stamp Act of 1765, suggested a year earlier by Grenville and meeting no very striking opposition then, imposed stamp duties on legal documents and on some luxury articles. These taxes were conventional, and heavier, in England, but they were imposed in America without the formal consent of the colonists, and would, in their eyes, aggravate the persistent lack of hard money. In Virginia this was especially irksome, and was made more difficult by the Currency Act of 1764, which made the colony's bills of credit no longer legal tender, and compelled her to withdraw from circulation those issued during the war.

Washington was only mildly aroused by the Stamp Act crisis and by the Resolves, submitted by Patrick Henry, that only the Virginia General Assembly had the right to tax Virginians. He expressed less apprehension than his old comrade of Braddock's expedition, Thomas Gage, now Lieutenant-General and the British commander in North America, to whom the Virginia Resolves "gave the signal for a general outcry over the continent". Washington's language to his London agents was restrained : "the speculative part of the Colonists . . . look upon this unconstitutional method of taxation as a direful attack upon their liberties, and loudly exclaim against the violation; what may be the result of this, and some other (I think I may add) ill-judged measures, I will not undertake to determine. . . ." He looked at the matter in practical terms, not as a matter of "right". Britain would gain much less than she anticipated from the tax, since in a crisis the "necessaries of life" could be found in America. "This will introduce frugality and be a necessary

45

stimulation to industry." In any event, the money was not available to buy the stamps. And "if a stop be put to our judicial proceedings I fancy the merchants of Great Britain trading to the Colonies will not be among the last to wish for a repeal of it".

Nevertheless, the prospect of no ships being cleared, no debts collected and no legal business transacted because the colony refused to countenance the use of the stamps did bring alarm; it was one of the reasons, though only one, why no tobacco was grown on the Potomac in 1766 and why Washington was planning and planting more varied crops. At Norfolk the Sons of Liberty resolved to use "all lawful ways and means" to preserve the right of "being taxed by none but representatives of their own choosing, and of being tried only by a jury of their own peers". A network of such clubs spread through the colonies, encouraged by Boston and New York merchants and lawyers. A colonial boycott of British goods began.

But the factors hinted at by Washington had more effect in securing the repeal of the Act than any threats of pressures in the colony: the persuasions of Benjamin Franklin at the bar of the House of Commons, and pleas like those of the London merchant Capel Hanbury, with whom Washington did business, brought the change. Hanbury said bluntly that neither Virginia nor Maryland had enough specie to pay the stamp tax and, an even more pertinent argument, if the Act remained in force he would be willing to sell his American accounts for half their face value. In the extravagant declarations of relief and of loyalty that greeted the news of repeal, the warning Declaratory Act, which passed the Commons unanimously and asserted Parliament's right to "bind the colonies in all cases whatsoever", was little heeded. Washington expressed a general sentiment: "All . . . who were instrumental in procuring the repeal are entitled to the thanks of every British subject and have mine cordially."

With the next stage in the argument, Washington became more involved. In 1767 the Townshend Acts had been passed, placing import duties on paints, glass, many kinds of paper and on tea. The proceeds of these were to be devoted to the strengthening of a centrally-controlled customs system and to the compensation of governors and judges.

Unlike the Stamp Act, these were external taxes, and hitherto few had denied the right of Parliament to impose external
taxes. They were designed, however, not to regulate trade,
but to collect a revenue, and, as the Virginia Assembly protested, "to compel the Colonists to part with their money
against their inclinations, your memorialists conceive to
be a tax internal to all intents and purposes". The cynic
might feel that by 1768 what was coming to constitute
tyranny was not the levying of the tax but its collection.
What was really feared, however, was that this revenue
would free colonial governors from the control of colonial
assemblies. The argument was gradually being put on constitutional grounds : to the British Parliament, the colonial
assemblies were local and subordinate; to the colonists, who
were not and could not be represented at Westminster, the
right of taxation must rest exclusively in the colonial legislative bodies. Colonial charters might appear to be merely
royal grants, but, in the colonists' view, they were coming to
be regarded as constitutions and social compacts. The colonists must not be held, in being colonists, to have forfeited
their "rights". The rights they claimed were still of course
the rights of Englishmen, not of Americans. Independence
seemed remote and unlikely.

In February 1768 the Massachusetts General Court issued
a "Circular Letter" appealing to the other colonies for
united action. This provoked a high-handed reply from
Lord Hillsborough, the holder of the new office of Secretary
of State for the Colonies, which aroused America more than
the letter itself. Virginia, which had sent representatives
neither to the Albany Congress to discuss inter-colonial
affairs in 1754 nor to the "Stamp Act Congress" in New
York in 1765, responded and supported Massachusetts in
1768. John Dickinson wrote his *Letters of a Pennsylvania
Farmer*, denouncing all taxation, internal or external, imposed by the British Parliament. Washington records that he
bought a copy. A new motif was introduced : a groping and
uncertain effort to stand together against what appeared to
be a fixed policy of control from above and from outside. If
to-day it is hard to see in the hesitant steps and often contradictory measures of Grenville and Rockingham, Townshend and North, anything as consistent as a "policy", never-

theless colonial fears of the British Parliament were steadily mounting.

From March 1768 onwards merchants in the northern colonies were making agreements not to import British goods. This appeal reached Washington in 1769, and he wrote to his neighbour and early adviser on farming, George Mason of Gunston Hall:

"At a time when our lordly Masters in Great Britain will be satisfied with nothing less than the deprication of American freedom, it seems highly necessary that something should be done to avert the stroke and maintain the liberty which we had derived from our ancestors; but the manner of doing it to answer the purpose effectually is the point in question.

"That no man should scruple or hesitate a moment to use a-ms in defence of so valuable a blessing, on which all the good and evil of life depends, is clearly my opinion; yet A-ms, I would beg leave to add, should be the last resource, the denier resort."

This, too, was a new and ugly note, and it represents Washington's first direct participation in the controversy with Britain. In 1769 he presented to the House of Burgesses a set of Resolves drawn up by Mason, declaring that the colonial assemblies had the sole right to impose taxes, and threatening a boycott. Both he and Mason recognised that the scattered nature of plantation life and the lack of manufactures, particularly of cloth, would make this far less effective in the southern colonies than in New England. But when the new Governor, the Scots-born Lord Dunmore, dissolved the Virginia Assembly in May 1769 because of its protests at British policy, the Burgesses moved into the Raleigh Tavern, and there formed an Association to enforce non-importation. Washington was elected to the committee to prepare the plan. It did something to foster the self-sufficient activities in the weaving-room and the smithy at Mount Vernon, but, in contrast to New England and New York, where trade was cut by at least half, it was not particularly successful in Virginia. It was welcomed by the smaller planters as a means of getting out of debt, but un-popular with those who lived "gentealy and hospitably, on clear Estates". In July 1771 the Association was dissolved, except for the ban on those articles still taxed to raise revenue. Since all the Townshend duties except that on tea had been repealed in April 1770, the edge of the issue seemed to have been dulled. New York denounced non-importation, and it was gradually abandoned. Where it remained in force, it was evaded by smuggling, as in New England.

Edmund Pendleton and many of the larger planters in Virginia had opposed the non-importation scheme from the beginning. There was emerging a certain fear of the radical position that Patrick Henry and Thomas Jefferson in Virginia, and James Otis and Sam Adams in Boston, were taking. The notion of economic independence of Britain and the development of colonial manufactures was more appealing to New England than to the plantations, whose economy, however perilous, was geared to the tobacco monopoly of the home market. Further, to colonial statesmen as skilled as Pendleton in Virginia or John Dickinson in Pennsylvania, and to many of their more loyalist-minded friends, threats of violence were personally distasteful and were deemed politically unwise : they would induce a stronger action on both sides and weaken the chances of conciliation. To base the argument on "rights" was to open the door, in the colonies as in Europe, to curious incomers. What was needed was what Governor Hutchinson described, in 1771, as "a little discreet conduct on both sides".

George Mason, on the other hand, thought non-importation did not go far enough. He wanted an agreement binding on all the colonies to ban the import of "articles of luxury and ostentation" and the encouragement of the movement of industries from Europe to the New World. Washington avoided both these extremes. He advocated the most binding non-importation agreements—"I could wish it to be ten times as strict"—and he was loyal to the Association so long as it offered a prospect of success. Once it failed, there was no place for sentimentality or for recrimination. The day it was abandoned he sent off an elaborate invoice for new clothes : it looked as if Jacky Custis, whom his tutor considered "exceedingly indolent" and "surprisingly voluptuous", and who had been pleading with his stepfather for a dark crimson dress suit lined with velvet, a pearl-coloured half-dress suit and "sundry modish waistcoats and breeches", would get them, after all.

Throughout the controversy, Washington's mind moved more slowly than those of many of his colleagues. Decisions in Virginia were made by an inner group of wealthy Tidewater planters, and Mason himself recognised that policy was "conducted and prepared with a great deal of privacy, and by very few members, of whom Patrick Henry is the principal". With the abandonment of non-importation, and with Lord North's repeal of all but the tea duty, there was a new optimism in the air, and for two years the revolutionary movement lost its momentum. The so-called Boston Massacre had little effect on Virginia, though the attack by Rhode Island smugglers on the British revenue cutter *Gaspée*, and the talk of sending those who were implicated to stand their trial in Britain, did cause some concern, and Dabney Carr, brother-in-law of Jefferson, persuaded the Virginian Assembly to appoint a Committee of Correspondence. This, said Sam Adams, would gladden "the hearts of all who are friends of liberty". Lord Dunmore thought that the resolves did "show a little ill-humour"—but planned a trip with Washington to the West to prospect for land.

Nor did the Boston Tea Party mar the all but tranquil mood of Virginia. For Massachusetts, however, it was a major step along the road to revolution. The attempt to relieve the East India Company of its surplus tea by allowing it to sell direct to the colonists was an ingenious device. The tea would be cheap—cheaper, indeed, than at home—and the only charge on it would be the hateful $3d.$ per pound tax; the smuggling rings importing Dutch tea would be broken; non-importation would now be difficult to enforce; and the British Parliament's right to compel the payment of a tax that by now had become symbolic would be vindicated. For one million Americans, it was estimated, drank tea twice daily; it was "the Idol of America", and cheap tea would quench the thirst for patriotism. The attack on the merchants' profits, however, forced them into an uneasy alliance with Sam Adams and his Sons of Liberty; New York and Philadelphia, which outdid Boston as smugglers' strongholds, outdid it, too, in protests; more orthodox businessmen joined in the fight against the Company *qua* monopo-

list; and a most intriguing propaganda campaign was unleashed against "that bane to America, that poison to
health", the East India Company's tea. Coffee drinking
became patriotic, and the "Tea Deum" culminated in the
pitching of 342 chests of the innocent Oriental herb into
Boston harbour. In the spirit of a Harvard Commencement,
the Sons of Liberty were somewhat casually dressed as
Indians; no one interfered with their fun, but what they
commenced was a revolution. Yet there was little stir in
Virginia, where there was no particular sympathy for the
sufferings of the merchant class. There was no reference to
the affair in any extant letter of Washington's for six months.

Britain took the high spirits of Boston more seriously and
abandoned her efforts at appeasement. "The spirit of riot"
was no novelty in the eighteenth century at home or abroad,
and it had flourished in the colonies largely because there
were so few troops to suppress it. By 1774, however, London
had had enough, especially of Boston—"obstinate, undutiful
and ungovernable from the very beginning". The colonists
lost the sympathy of the British merchant class, until now
largely on their side. The Intolerable Acts were passed in the
summer of 1774 : the Port of Boston was closed; the charter
of Massachusetts was revised and the Governor was given
the right to appoint officials; the number of troops under
Gage was increased, and, in the wake of these measures, the
Quebec Act was passed, transferring the area between the
Ohio and the Mississippi to the Province of Quebec and
bringing to it French civil law and the Roman Catholic
religion. The patriots could now smell Popery as well as
tyranny in every tainted breeze.

Virginians saw in these measures the prelude to an attack
on other colonial charters and on other civil liberties, an
attack indeed on the "liberty of North America"—the
phrase recurs repeatedly in a novel and striking way. A day
of prayer and fasting was proclaimed. The Assembly was
again dissolved by the Governor and again reconvened in
Anthony Hays' thriving tavern, from which, through the
Committee of Correspondence, a call for a Continental Congress was issued. The formalities of good behaviour, however, were honoured : the Burgesses gave a ball for Lady
Dunmore, newly arrived in the colony, and Washington, not

yet, if ever, a revolutionary, dined and breakfasted and talked about Western land with the Governor. But a decisive step had been taken, by Washington as by most of his fellow Burgesses. The Boston Port Act led him and them seriously to consider complete independence from Britain.

After discussions in their counties, they reconvened as Delegates, not Burgesses, in a Convention in Williamsburg in August 1774. Washington presented the Fairfax County Resolves, largely Mason's handiwork; they agreed to cease importing British goods; unless their grievances were redressed before August 1775, they undertook to ban the export of tobacco and all other products to Britain; and they chose seven Delegates who were to attend the General Congress to be held in Philadelphia in September. They were, first, their own Convener, the Speaker of their Assembly, the massive and genial Peyton Randolph; second, the scholar-radical Richard Henry Lee, and third, George Washington. The other four were Patrick Henry, "moderate and mild and in religious matters a Saint, but ye very Devil in Politicks"; the staunch Richard Bland, "with ye look of musty old Parchme'ts w'ch he handleth and studieth much"; the corpulent and gouty Benjamin Harrison, and Edmund Pendleton, the orphan who had made his own way in the world and who spoke for moderation. It was a strong and varied team—"the most spirited and consistent of any" said John Adams. Washington was the least eloquent of them all, but the most impressive in stature, the most experienced in war, and one of the most successful in the arts of men—and plantation—management. He did not go to Philadelphia in passion. Roger Atkinson, writing of the Delegates in October 1774, described him as "a modest man, but sensible and speaks little—in action cool, like a Bishop at his prayers". His modesty and his determination are apparent in his letter to Bryan Fairfax. The measures taken in London were, he held, "repugnant to every principle of natural justice; whilst much abler heads than my own hath fully convinced me that it is not only repugnant to natural right, but subversive of the law and constitution of Great Britain itself. . . ." On the 31st August 1774, in company with Pendleton and Henry, he was ferried over the Potomac and rode away to Philadelphia.

Chapter Four

Delegate and Patriot: The Continental Congresses (1774—1775)

SHORTLY before the First Continental Congress met, John Adams noted in his diary :

"There is one ugly reflection. Brutus and Cassius were conquered and slain. Hampden died in the field, Sidney on the scaffold, Harrington in jail, Etc. This is cold comfort."

Stirred either by the political excitements of the Congress, which was attended by fifty-five delegates, from every colony except Georgia, or by the feasting and festivity—"a most sinful feast again. . . . Wines most excellent and admirable. I drank Madeira at a great rate . . ."—Adams' Diary soon reflects a new note.

"There is in the Congress a collection of the greatest men upon this Continent in point of abilities, virtues and fortunes. The magnanimity and public spirit which I see here make me blush for the sordid, venal herd which I have seen in my own Province . . . All the seven delegates of Virginia are here and more sensible fine fellows you would never wish to see . . ."

It is clear that, though the moderates were in control, Virginia and South Carolina brought a great reinforcement of strength to the New England radicals. Gadsden of South Carolina urged an immediate attack on the British in Boston before their troops could be reinforced. Richard Henry Lee proposed a total boycott. Peyton Randolph of Virginia became president of the Congress. Silas Deane of Connecticut was also impressed by the Virginians, "sociable, sensible and spirited", and particularly by Washington—"nearly as tall a man as Colonel Fitch, and almost as hard a countenance, yet with a very young look, and an easy, soldier-like air and gesture."

Contemporary verses by Dr. Solomon Drowne show that Washington wore his uniform and sword at the meetings in the Carpenters' Hall, and that his physical presence, six foot two and "as straight as an Indian", was beginning to exert influence.

> *"With manly gait*
> *His faithful steel suspended by his side,*
> *Passed W—shi—gt—n along, Virginia's Hero."*

In debate, however, he was completely silent. When Henry was crying out that government was dissolved and the distinctions between colonies were no more—"I am not a Virginian but an American"—Washington was more cautious. John Adams noted his common sense. When Richard Henry Lee and others thought that in time Britain would yield, recall her troops and withdraw her Acts, "Washington only", he said, "was in doubt".

"He never spoke in public. In private he joined with those who advocated a non-exportation, as well as a non-importation agreement. With both he thought we should prevail, without either he thought it doubtful. Henry was clear in one opinion, Richard Henry Lee in an opposite opinion, and Washington doubted between the two."

He saw the position of the colonies more clearly than most. Non-importation was necessary but difficult to enforce; non-exportation might bring Britain to terms, but it could ruin America in the process. And the southern colonies, Virginia with its tobacco, North Carolina with its naval stores and South Carolina with its rice and indigo, needed the British and European trade even more than Pennsylvania or New England. At one stage, four South Carolinian delegates withdrew from the Congress, and their adherence to the Association was obtained in the end only by permitting the export of rice to Europe. In its final form the Association was similar to that adopted in Virginia. British goods, especially East India tea, were not to be imported after 1st December 1774. As for non-exportation, that was suspended because of "the earnest desire we have, not to injure our fellow-subjects in Great Britain, Ireland or the West Indies". If the obnoxious Acts were not repealed by September 1775, then all exports to Britain were to be cut off—except South Carolina's rice to Europe. Frugality and home industry were to be encouraged; extravagance and dissipation—horse-racing and gaming—to be discontinued. Committees of "safety and inspection", aided by ostracism, "infamy" and tar and feathers, were the instruments of persuasion.

The Association was not a satisfactory weapon of coercion, and it showed that the colonists were already facing sectional as well as constitutional and personal rivalries. Moreover, the Congress was too nicely balanced between moderates and radicals for an agreed and compelling programme to emerge. The delegates, Adams noted, were "one-third Tories, another Whigs, and the rest Mongrels". If Lee and Henry and the "wild men" of Massachusetts were prominent in debate, there were others pleading for caution, like Pendleton of Virginia, John Jay of New York and John Dickinson and Joseph Galloway of Pennsylvania. Of these Galloway was the most explicit and the most austere. He sought redress of grievances and the restoration of harmony with Britain, and denounced the Association as a menace to law and liberty. He put forward a *Plan of a proposed Union between Great Britain and the Colonies*: a statesmanlike paper providing for an American legislature within the Empire with the title of "Grand Council", elected by all the colonies and acting as an inferior branch of the Home Parliament. Though it won the support of the middle colonies, it did not have that of Massachusetts or of the more vocal Virginians. The plan, with all that it might have done for Anglo-American and Imperial relations then and since, was defeated by one vote.

In the end, a Declaration of Rights and Grievances was drawn up : it denied the justice of taxation without representation as the infringement of a natural right and demanded the repeal of the Intolerable Acts. A petition was sent to the King, their "Most Gracious Sovereign", pleading that he dismiss from office "designing and dangerous men" (and, incidentally, reviling Catholicism in extended Quebec). An appeal was sent to Quebec to rise against British tyranny and to join a Congress called for the following year (diplomatically omitting all reference to Catholicism). And a series of Resolves (the Suffolk Resolves) were endorsed, denying any obligation to obey recent Acts of Parliament, and hinting, if all else failed, at armed resistance. This Congress was the most representative and significant of intercolonial assemblies so far; it had assumed the right to speak for all the colonies, and it set in motion a number of effective local machines. But it was not agreed on policy, it was not yet belligerent and it was not yet republican in mood. The King was still recognised as the binding element in the Empire. As Washington put it himself, in a letter to his old friend of the French wars, Captain Robert Mackenzie, then serving under Gage in Boston—as for Independency "and what not . . . I am well satisfied, that no such thing is desired by any thinking man in all North America".

If in the debates Washington played a minor role, his stature grew. He was by repute a man of courage and of wealth; he wore his uniform proudly; and it was reported that, on hearing in the House of Burgesses in Virginia of the passing of the Boston Port Bill, he had offered to raise and arm and lead a thousand men at his own expense. Moreover, his judgment was trusted. "Col. Washington, who has no pretensions to eloquence, is a man of more solid judgment and information than any man on that floor," said Henry. And, unlike Adams, Washington's diary shows him active and at ease socially : it tells indeed not of the measures of the Congress but of dining at the tavern with Bostonians and Pennsylvanians; few card games and no horse-racing apparently, but there was tea, licit or otherwise, with Mrs. Roberdeau, and the official welcome by the city, with music and guns and thirty-six toasts, to the King, the Queen, the Prince of Wales, and "The Perpetual Union of the Colonies".

The Congress left the door open for conciliation, but neither side was willing to give way. As "timid" a man as John Dickinson had no doubts—"The first act of violence on the part of administration in America, or the attempt to re-inforce General Gage this winter or next year will put the whole continent in arms, from Nova Scotia to Georgia . . . a determined and unanimous resolution animates this continent." The King and his Ministers were equally determined, if the country was less unanimous. Yet the elections for the new Parliament that met in November 1774 showed popular support for coercion. The speech from the throne noted the "disobedience to law" in Massachusetts and expressed the royal resolution to maintain "the supreme authority of this Legislature over all the Dominions of my Crown, the maintenance of which I consider as essential to the dignity, the safety and the welfare of the British Empire". Chatham's proposals in the Lords in January 1775, to recall troops from Boston and to impose no taxes for revenue purposes without the consent of the colonial assemblies, were defeated. Despite these portents, the hope of compromise died slowly in Virginia—". . . by private letters from London", wrote Washington on 25th February, "there is reason to believe the ministry would willingly change their ground". One of his informants was George Fairfax, who had written: "you are condemned by the M——y, and their dependants, and much Aplauded by every Welwisher to the Antient and Constitutional Right of Englishmen, whether on this, or the other side of the Atlantic . . ."

The confidence of correspondents and of merchants was unfounded. In February 1775 the North Government offered to go back to the custom of requesting assemblies to appropriate funds when needed, but accompanied this tentative proposal with reprisals. The New England Restraining Act of March was passed, denying the New England colonies the right to fish off the Grand Banks and confining their trade to Britain, Ireland and the British West Indies. "As the Americans had refused to trade with this Kingdom, it was but just that we should not suffer them to trade with any other nation."

It was in the discussion on this measure that Burke made his memorable plea for conciliation—but to empty benches. As if to mark the moment of decision, it was on the day following, in Richmond, Virginia, in the Virginian Convention which had been summoned by Peyton Randolph, that Henry offered uglier counsel, and proposed that "this Colony be immediately put in a posture of defence. . . . I know not what course others may take; but as for me, give me liberty or give me death!"

The change of mood in the colonies was very marked after October 1774, when Washington returned from Philadelphia. The Association was being enforced. British exports to the colonies fell dramatically. The production of local goods increased, and self-interest came to buttress patriotism. By the end of the year, ten colonies had provincial congresses, extra-legal, but largely composed of the same men as sat in the assemblies. Dunmore wrote anxiously to the Earl of Dartmouth that every county was on a war footing. Independent companies were being organised and drilled, and, though slowly, armed. Even before Washington left Philadelphia the Fairfax County Company had inquired if he could obtain for them ". . . a pair of colors, two drums and two fifes and two halberts", and they had, significantly, asked whether the colours should vary from those carried by regulars or militia. In the next few months Washington was offered the command of seven of these county companies. He knew full well how erratic a force militia was, and urged the training of special companies of riflemen, to wear hunting shirts.

On 20th March, 1775, as a representative of Fairfax, he attended the Virginian Convention which Peyton Randolph summoned to meet in Richmond, at a safe remove from the Governor and his warships. It was, in fact, indistinguishable from a meeting of the Burgesses, except that it was more fully representative—all the counties sent delegates. The only absentee was the Burgess for the College of William and Mary—Attorney-General John Randolph, brother of Peyton, was a Loyalist. He was to leave Virginia with Dunmore, and to die in poverty in Scotland. Prominent in the Convention were westerners with military experience, like Thomas Walker and Washington's old comrades, Adam Stephen and Andrew Lewis, fresh from his victory over the Indians at Point Pleasant. The proceedings of the Philadelphia Congress were unanimously approved. On Henry's motion, the Convention agreed to prepare its defences, and Washington, along with Stephen and Lewis, served on the committee to consider how this might be done. They proposed, and the Convention agreed, that each of the counties on and east of the fall-line should raise one or more troops of cavalry, thirty men to the troop; the other counties were each to raise at least one foot company of sixty-eight rank and file. Since the major weakness would be the lack of ammunition and equipment, each county was to levy a head tax for the purchase of ammunition. The seven delegates to the First Continental Congress were re-elected to serve as delegates to the Second, summoned for May; Washington this time second only to Peyton Randolph and ahead of Henry. As the crisis approached and military questions became primary, his role became more important; and as it grew, so did his stature and his patience. In the work of the Richmond Convention the Rubicon seems to have been crossed. As he wrote to his brother on 25th March—"it is my full intention to devote my life and fortune in the cause we are engaged in, if need be".

April was still more decisive. On 27th April Washington first heard the news of Governor Dunmore's seizure of the powder from the magazine in Williamsburg known as the "Horn", an octagonal building, now carefully preserved, which hardly looks large enough to be, in fact, the scene of the outbreak of the Revolution in Virginia. Fourteen troops of light horse, six hundred men in all, assembled in Fredericksburg, and Henry put himself at the head of the Hanover County militia. By Peyton Randolph's efforts trouble was for a time averted—violence, he said, confusedly but prophetically, "may produce effects which God only knows the effects of".

Violence had, in fact, already occurred, though neither Randolph nor Washington knew it. The embattled farmers of Massachusetts had, at Concord bridge, fired the shot heard round the world. Alarmed by the reports that the Provincial Congress was collecting stores at Concord, and under orders from home to seize the ringleaders of rebellion, General Gage, now Military Governor of Massachusetts, decided to raid the store-house and perhaps by a show of force to avert the incipient revolution. A British force of about eight hundred grenadiers and light infantrymen was ferried from Boston to Charlestown on the night of 18th April 1775, and set off on a night march for Concord, eighteen miles away. Before it reached Lexington, where it hoped to arrest Sam Adams and John Hancock, William Dawes and Paul Revere had roused the minutemen, and at dawn on the 19th April seventy militia were drawn up on Lexington Green. No one knows who gave the order to fire, but in the skirmish that followed eight militia were killed and ten wounded. The British troops pushed on to Concord and destroyed those stores not already removed; then, after a fight at Concord bridge, they began their long march back to Boston, sniped at all the way. They reached Boston only with the help of reinforcements under

Lord Percy, and lost 273 men, three times more than the colonists. The colonial militia, reinforced from all New England, closed in around the city and began a siege.

When Washington and his colleagues reached Philadelphia on 9th May, they were welcomed by the leading citizens and the officers of the military companies, by a band and an escort of riflemen. Their welcome was outmatched by that shown the New England delegates the next day, for at their head were Hancock and Adams, now fugitives from the British redcoats, and given the reception accorded to heroes. The sixty-three delegates knew each other now; they had all been chosen by radical and extra-legal conventions; they represented all thirteen colonies, though not East or West Florida, Quebec or Nova Scotia. And the news from the north produced a speed, a resolution and an enthusiasm hitherto absent. "There never appeared more perfect unanimity among any set of men," said Richard Henry Lee. Benjamin Franklin, freshly returned from London and as delegate replacing Galloway, now an avowed Loyalist, found "all America from one End of the 12 United Provinces to the other, busily employed in learning the Use of Arms . . . the Unanimity is amazing". Samuel Curwen the Loyalist was depressed by the Second Congress—"I could not perceive the least disposition to accomodate matters."

This was not quite true. There were still some delegates, like John Dickinson, who urged caution and conciliation, and the Congress adopted Dickinson's "Olive Branch" petition— which the King refused to receive and which London denounced as an "insult and mockery". The majority were still against independence, but were convinced that they must support Massachusetts. The Congress resolved that the "colonies be immediately put into a state of defence". The British, or, as they carefully described it, the "Ministerial", Army must be resisted even as loyalty to the King was expressed. The hope was still of compelling concessions by compelling a change of Ministry—"that a speedy end may be put to the civil discords". But there was a clear recognition of the need for force. New York was instructed to send 5,000 barrels of flour to the Continental Army, and all the colonies were to send saltpetre and brimstone to be made into powder. Congress authorised the raising of ten companies of "expert riflemen" from Pennsylvania, Maryland and Virginia to march to Boston. On 6th July 1775, almost exactly a year before the Declaration of Independence, the Congress issued its "Declaration of Causes of Taking Up Arms", justifying resistance by force to "the tyranny of irritated ministers". "Oh that I were a soldier," said John Adams. "I will be. I am reading military books. Everyone must and will and shall be a soldier." Writing to Fairfax, Washington expressed not joy but horror at the prospect of fraternal conflict. "But can a virtuous man hesitate in his choice?"

With Peyton Randolph in the chair and secrecy surrounding their deliberations, the Congress began to act as a colonial parliament. The problems of 1775 were now of tactics rather than of strategy, and, indeed, military matters came rapidly to the foremost place. Dr. Joseph Warren, President of the newly-constituted and illegal "Provincial Congress of Massachusetts", bluntly told the Continental Congress:

"We have . . . passed a unanimous resolve for thirteen thousand six hundred men, to be forthwith raised by this Colony. . . . We beg leave to suggest that a powerful army on the side of America hath been considered by (Massachusetts) as the only means left to stem the rapid progress of a tyrannical ministry."

While the Congress was considering this plainly revolutionary proposal, Patrick Henry arrived belatedly from Virginia, full of his role in countering the Governor, of the proclamation ordering his (Henry's) arrest, and of the armed guard his supporters had gleefully provided him across the state on his way north. On the 24th May, Peyton Randolph left the Congress to preside over the session of the Virginian General Assembly Dunmore had at length called. It was the last Washington was to see of this ox-like, shrewd and amiable man. On the 5th June, Dunmore took refuge on H.M.S. *Fowey*, and for the next few months attacked Virginian coastal towns and destroyed Norfolk. Peyton Randolph presided over the third Convention in Richmond, which appointed a general "committee of safety" headed by Edmund Pendleton, and which became the effective government of the state. Dunmore sailed home in defeat in July 1776; Peyton Randolph returned to Philadelphia, where he died in October 1775.

But Washington's eyes were turned north by that time. As war approached, he was given formidable assignments as head of committees, first to plan the defence of New York, second to consider ways and means of obtaining ammunition and supplies, third to prepare regulations for the army. Events were now outrunning strategy, in the north as in Virginia. Ethan Allen, at the head of the Green Mountain Boys, temporarily abandoned his war with Governor Tryon of New York, who had put a price on his head, and captured the totally unprepared Forts Ticonderoga and Crown Point at the northern end of Lake George, and with them some valuable artillery. Allen won immortality by summoning the commander at Ticonderoga to surrender "in the name of the great Jehovah, and the Continental Congress", two authorities he himself never fully recognised. The New York folk-version of the summons is less eloquent—"Come out," he shouted, "you damned old rat." As he told it himself:

"The sun seemed to rise that morning with a superior luster, and Ticonderoga and its dependencies smiled on its conquerors, who tossed about the flowing bowl, and wished success to Congress and the Liberty and freedom of America."

Congress was less pleased by his success than he was himself. For this operation was on the Vermonters' initiative, and Congress could justify it only by claiming that Britain was preparing to invade the American colonies from Quebec as a base.

To these problems were added requests for guidance from Massachusetts: what should the colony do about the establishment of civil authority, what of supplies and money, and had not the time come for Congress to assume general direction of the unwieldy army assembling in the colony? Quite a number of delegates felt it was long overdue. Artemas Ward was commanding the troops in front of Boston. Some New England delegates supported him for the general command, some favoured others equally familiar with the situation in the north. But John Adams, one of the most respected of the northern delegates, had been impressed in both Continental Congresses by Washington. "Colonel Washington appears at Congress in his uniform," he noted on 29th May, "and by his great experience and abilities in military matters, is of much service to us." The buff and blue of the Fairfax Company had marked Washington out from the beginning; it suggested a man with his mind made up.

It is clear from his committee assignments that Washington was regarded in the Congress as the military expert, however slight his experience and whatever his own protestations. He did not once "insinuate"—his own word—that he wanted the command. It has even been argued that Pendleton's opposition in the Congress to the nomination of Washington was at Washington's own instigation, though David Mays, Pendleton's latest biographer, suggests that Pendleton was afraid of committing Virginia to the radical courses of Boston.

There were other candidates : Putnam, Heath, Ward, Arnold were New England possibilities. Gerry, Sam Adams and Joseph Warren of Massachusetts and R. H. Lee of Virginia favoured Charles Lee, the British regular on half-pay who had fought in Poland and Portugal and was now buying land in Berkeley County, Virginia, and being treated as a military expert. He had visited Mount Vernon in the winter of 1774 and discussed the situation—and borrowed £15. They thought that if he was unacceptable because not American born, then "the beloved Colonel Washington" was the man. There were other claimants in Virginia itself, in Colonel William Byrd of Westover, who had succeeded Washington as Virginian commander-in-chief, and in Andrew Lewis, who had as good a record in battle as any, and was now chasing Dunmore from the Tidewater. He was, however, taciturn in manner and without Washington's social claims.

Washington had shown knowledge of military matters in committee, and had been tested by adversity as well as by success on the frontier; he had shown caution and judgment, patience and self-possession; he had a sense of business; he was a delegate, familiar with his fellows and with the politics of war. He was acceptable to moderates and to militants. And to these Adams added the telling point that he was a Virginian and a man of means; it would be a master stroke to associate a Virginian planter with a war that might be thought to be thus far largely a New England, and a Radical, enterprise.

When on 14th June Adams mentioned his name to the Congress, it was a dramatic moment : John Hancock, then Speaker, and proscribed as an arch-rebel by the King's Ministers, had half hoped for the nomination himself; Adams alluded, however, to one with skill and experience as an officer, and, significantly, with an independent fortune, a gentleman from Virginia. Washington slipped from the room before the discussion became embarrassing and before Samuel Adams seconded his cousin. The discussion on the 14th had no conclusion. There were no extravagant estimates of Washington's ability. As Eliphalet Dyer wrote to Joseph Trumbull—"He is a gentleman highly esteemed by those acquainted with him, though I don't believe, as to his military and real service, he knows more than some of ours but so it removes all jealousies. . . ." Dyer thought he was "discreet and Virtuous, no Rarum Starum ranting Swearing fellow, but Sober, steady and Calm".

On the 15th Congress resolved "that a General be appointed to command all the continental forces, raised, or to be raised, for the defence of American liberty". Washington was proposed formally by Thomas Johnson of Maryland, his associate in the Potomac navigation project, and election was unanimous. On the 16th June he accepted the commission, refusing, however, to accept any salary, and declaring "with the utmost sincerity, I do not think myself equal to the Command I am honoured with". He kept careful account of his expenses, and at the end of the war transcribed them carefully into a ledger headed "Dr. The United States . . . in account with—G : Washington Cr."

His selection clearly did not surprise Washington. Writing to his brother he avowed that "the partiallity of the Congress joined to a political motive, really left me without a choice". His letter to Martha on the 18th confirms it—"I was apprehensive I could not avoid this appointment." Equally there is no reason to doubt the sincerity of his protests :

"I have used every endeavour in my power to avoid it, not only from my unwillingness to part with you and the family, but from a consciousness of its being a trust too great for my capacity, and that I should enjoy more real happiness in one month with you at home than I have the most distant prospect of finding abroad, if my stay were to be seven times seven years. But it has been a kind of destiny that has thrown me upon this service. . . . It was utterly out of my power to refuse this appointment, without exposing my character to such censure as would have reflected dishonor upon myself, and have given pain to my friends. This, I am sure, could not, and ought not to be pleasing to you, and must have lessened me considerably in my own esteem. I shall rely, therefore, confidently on that Providence which has heretofore preserved and been bountiful to me, not doubting but that I shall return safe to you in the fall. . . ."

To Burwell Bassett he put it more objectively—"I can answer but for three things, a firm belief in the justice of our cause, close attention to the prosecution of it, and the strictest integrity."

And to Henry, more trenchantly and with a sharp gambler's sense of the risks he ran—"Remember, Mr. Henry, what I now tell you : from the day I enter upon the command of the American armies, I date my fall, and the ruin of my reputation."

He could be as gloomy and inaccurate a prophet as John Adams himself.

The more carefully the causes of the American Revolution are analysed, the more difficult it becomes to offer any brief and simple statement about them. The researches of Sir Lewis Namier and of Professor Richard Pares in Britain have demonstrated that the Whig view of the reign of George III as one in which an autocratic monarch sought to regain a lost prerogative and in so doing brought down an empire is no longer tenable. The American Revolution was due not to George's tyranny but to his Government's weakness and irresolution. Similarly two generations of American scholars, from C. M. Andrews, Charles Beard and Carl Becker to Professors Gipson and Hacker, Schlesinger Senior and J. C. Miller have made it clear that the old picture of gallant colonists struggling against political and economic tyranny, and dedicating their lives to the proposition that there should be no taxation without representation, is but a partial view of the many factors making for independence. Neither in Britain nor in America did the taxed have adequate representation : not one person in fifty in Britain had the vote—

one hundred and sixty thousand voters elected all the members of Parliament. Few members of Boston mobs and few workers on the plantations had the suffrage either. Nor did the colonists seek representation at Westminster : if taxation was necessary, it was to be imposed by their own, highly unrepresentative, assemblies.

There was little unanimity of opinion in the colonies. Not only did one-third of the colonists remain loyalist, including Lord Fairfax in the Valley, but even the more radical revolutionary leaders were slow to formulate a demand for independence. It had not yet been made when Washington took up arms. When the demand was voiced, by a far from representative Congress of precariously united states, it came at the end of two hectic years of thrust and parry, in which threats of coercion, declarations of resistance and pleas for conciliation were all haphazardly mixed. As late as August 1775, Jefferson still sought "dependence on Great Britain, properly limited". In the years from 1765 to 1773 there were few signs of imminent separation, and many pointers to the success of more moderate counsels.

Despairing of seeing a pattern in the years from 1774 to 1776, historians have looked less to the events that led to the Revolution than to its deeper and long-term causes. Nor does the latest research entirely support some well-established theses. Charles Beard and Louis Hacker, for instance, have maintained that the Revolution was primarily a conflict of mercantile and industrial interests between a mercantilist mother country and an expanding, a distant and an increasingly less English colony. Yet in 1774 the Continental Congress offered to maintain the navigation system if exempted from parliamentary taxation, and in 1775 Franklin offered to have all the fundamental Acts of Trade separately re-enacted by each colonial assembly—if only the parliamentary claim to the right to tax were dropped. It is certainly true that the struggle was as much over colonial manufactures and colonial products, over lands and furs, sugar and tea, as over constitutional concepts. But there is hardly any reference in the Declaration of Independence to the Acts of Trade : only one item among twenty-seven. It was redress of grievances rather than independence that even the merchants sought.

Many admirers of American Federalism and of the modern conception of the British Commonwealth have argued that the core of the dispute lay in the contemporary theory of the indivisibility of sovereignty and of the supremacy of Parliament, that had Joseph Galloway or Franklin, Francis Maseres or Adam Smith, been listened to, or had Pitt been in office and able to act the part of Lord Durham, Parliament's insistence on its right to tax as the very essence of sovereignty might have been modified and dominion Parliaments under a single monarch might have emerged. But the institution which appeared an oppressor to Americans was to Englishmen the protector of the liberties won in 1688; none of the great English Whigs of the day approved of imperial federation, nor of the enlargement of royal authority that it apparently implied. The King was still a real force in government and could not yet be a symbol of a wider Commonwealth.

J. F. Jameson, Carl Becker and James Truslow Adams have stressed the importance of the radicalism of western frontiersmen and artisans, as passionately for independence as any eastern merchant, but with totally different economic interests. This interpretation, for which there is perhaps more evidence in New York, Pennsylvania and the Carolinas than in Virginia, led Becker to use the phrase that the American Revolution was not only a struggle for Home Rule, it was also a question of who should rule at home, both in Britain and in America. This view, which sees the American Revolution as a class war that was also a frontier challenge, has been highly esteemed for forty years, yet it, too, is only partly true. New England radicalism was Boston-bred, and at least until the passing of the Quebec Act the "river gods" of the trans-Connecticut frontier were as often loyalist as patriot; four of the great estates in New York—Livingston and Morrisania, Cortlandt and Rensselaerswyck—provided Revolutionary not Loyalist leaders; the planters of Virginia, affluent in manner but short of ready cash, and with no love of the Scotch-Irish in the Valley or of the indentured servants on their Tidewater estates, were as a group Conservative in temper but Revolutionary in politics; the Highlanders on the North Carolina frontier who had fought for Stuart Prince Charlie at Culloden in '46 were fighting equally un-

successfully but no less gallantly for Hanoverian George III
at Moore's Creek Bridge in '76. In Maryland there was
hardly any frontier radicalism at all. The Revolution certainly unleashed a struggle of economic interests in the
colonies, but the pattern fluctuates from one colony to
another, and is shaped more by local than by "national"
factors.

If some older themes are now open to question, recent
research has emphasised two aspects of the Revolution that
reveal how "modern" an event it was. Philip Davidson has
shown that the coming of the Revolution was a triumph of
skilful propaganda : practically all the colonial newspapers
were Whig, and the American Revolution was one of the
first great popular movements in which the newspapers
played a vital part. "A curious employment," John Adams
described it, "cooking up paragraphs, articles and occur-
rences, etc., working the political engine." Newspapers were
especially important in enlisting the support of the farmers
behind a movement which began as a protest of the seaports
and the trading towns. They were especially necessary in
Virginia, for the absence of large towns, the dependence on
tobacco and the vulnerability of the scattered plantations to
attack weakened rather than strengthened the idea of separation from Britain.

Yet almost to a man the pamphleteers were Northerners :
Sam Adams and Josiah Quincy, Joseph Warren and James
Otis, Thomas Mifflin and Joseph Hawley. And they had the
help of one of the first advocates of international revolution
in modern history, Tom Paine. Through newspapers, tracts
and harangues, through the Sons of Liberty, the Mohawk
River Indians, the Philadelphia Patriotic Society and many
other groups, the radicals seized upon and exaggerated every
mistake the Home Government made and perfected the
machinery of revolution. Unlike the contemporary British
Press, they hardly ever printed a word sympathetic to the
Home Government or to Loyalists.

The studies of L. H. Gipson, L. A. Harper and O. M.
Dickerson have made clear how much the Revolution was
the offshoot of a world clash of competing empires and of
that recast and refurbished theory of Imperialism, that, in
Burke's words, made England appear "like a porcupine

armed all over with Acts of Parliament, oppressive to trade and America". What was particularly aggravating in colonial trade was not the Navigation Acts, which served as "the cement of Empire", but the methods and the corruption of British enforcing agents and revenue collectors after 1764.

Revolutions are never, of course, simple phenomena. The American Revolution is especially complex because of the scattered nature and the varied economies and populations of the thirteen colonies. There were few natural centres of resistance; if Boston was "mobbish" in its revolutionary sentiments, New York was oligarchic and plutocratic, and Philadelphia, which became the meeting-place of the Revolutionary Congress, was a Quaker city, where piety marched with profit and the Franklins spoke for all. There was no Paris to focus and marshal a nation's discontents. There was no one city or area which, if stormed or destroyed, would end the rebellion. Similarly there were pressures for independence, but rarely united pressure groups. The merchants were a powerful force for independence, it is true, but in New York in the French and Indian War they and the Governor of the colony had traded so freely with the enemy that the Iroquois complained; they continued in the Revolutionary War, as later in the Civil War, to see themselves as middle and neutral men. Pennsylvanians were similarly tempted. Virginia's and Maryland's merchants tended to be Tories. Among the Charleston merchants Loyalism was strong, though two of the wealthiest—Henry Laurens and Gabriel Manigault—were ardent patriots. Many Boston merchants did not become revolutionary until Lord North struck at their tea smuggling, nor did they ever make any very harmonious common cause with Liberty. Similarly, though many lawyers were Whigs, there were some who stayed Loyalist— William Smith in New York; Joseph Galloway, William Allen and Benjamin Chew in Philadelphia; John Randolph in Virginia.

If there was no one centre of rebellion and if the leaders were extraordinarily heterogeneous, nevertheless many tensions had arisen in all the colonies in the previous fifty years— from many causes. The population was doubling every twenty-five years. Waves of immigration were increasingly less English in stock—one-sixth of the population was Scotch-

Irish; there were 200,000 Germans. Religious revivalism was taking highly explosive and democratic forms, and to many the Anglican Church, and particularly the proposed American Episcopate, were "the halfway house to Rome"—"the sight of Lawn Sleeves . . . more terrible than ten thousand Mohawks". The religious provisions of the Quebec Act, not its territorial changes, caused excitement in the Tidewater. The size of the colonies made them of interest to Britain as markets as well as sources of raw materials just when they were beginning to have policies of their own devising. There was a growing search for economic self-sufficiency, a quest for foreign markets and foreign suppliers in the West Indies and in Europe, despite British Acts of Trade. Northern groups found that their developing industries did not harmonise with mercantilist theory. Southern groups, more English than the English in dress and manners and patriarchal in their ways, were increasingly suspicious of British political interference—and of Scots factors and Scots governors. Frontier areas became as suspicious of the East as of the British except when Indians raided. In all the colonies a new democratic sap was rising, half pioneer, half Puritan; assemblies were challenging and curbing royal or proprietary governors, and a vigorous public debate greeted every measure of policy from London. Indeed, the colonists enjoyed so much freedom and expressed it so bluntly that they were indignant when any small part of it was infringed. If the Revolution was a struggle for freedom from Britain, it was also an expression of freedom in the diversity of its causes and the range of its leadership in thirteen very diverse and distant colonies.

The Revolution reflected all of these strains and discontents, the growing pains of a new and restless society. But no one pattern of explanation holds of all the colonies. What can be said is that the disappearance from the western frontier of the torch and the tomahawk in 1763 released the tensions and removed the curbs. It did not make the Revolution inevitable, for there is no inevitability in history. Had George III and his Ministers been better informed and more imaginative, more resolute in action and less pedantic in manner, the break could have been at least postponed and perhaps averted. Since policy was, in the last resort, made in London, the responsibility for the coming of the Revolution must rest there. In the month when the First Continental Congress met, September 1774, even Burke thought "the American and foreign affairs will not come to any crisis". In the General Election of that year, American affairs were not prominent and North's Government had a comfortable majority. And British merchants, formerly so responsive to American bans on their imports, were cushioned against the blows of 1774 and 1775 by the sharp increase in exports to Spain, Italy and the East Indies. It is still sad to read the eloquent and deeply felt declarations of loyalty to the King offered by revolutionary leaders in Virginia as late as 1773 and 1774—Washington among them. But, however much loyalist sympathy there might be, the Home Government had failed to enforce its policy, and it failed to protect its customs officers, its stamp masters and its tea consignees from attack. In many provinces the legal machinery was inadequate; neither Grenville nor North foresaw trouble, nor had they plans for dealing with it; there were too few troops to keep order, just enough to provoke disorder. As Colonel Dalrymple, commanding the troops in Boston, said, "Government here is in the hands of the Multitude". And as Chief Justice Oliver added, "When Jove is distant, lightning is not to be feared". "The only crime we have been guilty of is the inconsistency of our policy," said Solicitor-General Wedderburn in 1775. "That has encouraged the mutinous subjects and dismayed the well affected in America. We have taught . . . the dangerous lesson that their turbulence had an influence upon our councils." Opinion hardened in 1774. After the passing of the Intolerable Acts, the range of manœuvre of Ministers and rebels was restricted, and events began to have a momentum of their own.

Washington and his "country" are good examples of these general statements. The initiative in the Revolution was provided by two colonies, Massachusetts and Virginia, outstanding in the size of their populations, in their wealth and in their cultural attainments. In neither was there a strong British force around which Loyalists could rally. Just as Gage's government in Boston controlled only the town itself and real power passed to a provincial congress in Salem and a Committee of Safety, so in Virginia Lord Dunmore's removal of gunpowder from Williamsburg and the threat of slave insurrections gave impetus and authority to the extra-legal convention sitting in Richmond. What was striking about Virginia was that the men of property and political prominence, unlike their counterparts in other colonies except Massachusetts, were almost unanimous in their support of the "patriotic" cause. But a handful apart—Henry, Jefferson, Mason, Dabney Carr, the Lees and a few more—the lords of the gauntlet and the glove were not by temperament revolutionary, as were, say, Sam Adams and Tom Paine.

The least revolutionary of them all was Washington. His cast of mind was practical and unquestioning. Unlike Mason and Jefferson, he has left no statement giving an intellectual justification for revolt; what survive are fugitive comments only, largely derivative from "abler heads". Nor are some frequently cited "causes" of the Revolution in Virginia as accurate in Washington's case as they are often held to be. The Proclamation Line of 1763 did not particularly alarm him; he regarded it as temporary, and he certainly showed no violent hostility to the government that enacted it. Though more than any other Virginian he had reason to feel aggrieved at the seniority rule applying to British as against colonial commissions, by 1774 he appeared to have forgotten his grievances of 1754–8; and, in any event, he had, with Braddock's aides as with Forbes, been held in high regard and been treated on his merits. No one liked London finery more than Washington or was a better customer of Messrs. Hanbury. By diversifying his crops, he was by 1770 less subject to the depressions that afflicted his fellow planters still dependent on tobacco; from the Custis property he had a wealth, and a credit, that saved him from the constant nagging of factors in Virginia and merchants in London. Patsy's death had allowed him to pay off much of his own debt to Robert Cary. Washington is thus innocent of the charge that he encouraged the Revolution in order to free himself of his debts. In all the discussions on non-importation in 1773 and 1774, he repeatedly emphasised that the break in trade with Britain must not be made the excuse for refusing to honour an obligation. "Whilst we are accusing others of injustice, we should be just ourselves, and how this can be, whilst we owe a considerable debt, and refuse payment of it to Great Britain, is to me inconceivable."

Why, then, a supporter of non-importation, a delegate to Philadelphia, and soon Commander-in-Chief of a rebel army? One explanation is that, behind the calm exterior and the preference for administration to theorising, there was immensely strong but tightly disciplined feeling. It erupted only occasionally in his letters—as it was to explode only occasionally in war. But it occurred with Hanbury in 1774, when the firm he had traded with for twenty years without ever seeing, queried a bill of exchange—it ended Washington's relations with them. No one as sensitive as Washington could enjoy the situation of dependence in which the planter found himself, over-charged for goods, often of shoddy quality and often ill-fitting, and with no redress. What angered him and his colleagues was not the mercantile system, but its abuse; not indebtedness and the pledging of their uncertain crops, but exploitation.

The roots of his revolutionary leadership were deeper than this : they lay in land and in loyalty. Washington by training and by his position on the middle Potomac was the most Western-minded of Tidewater planters, owning more land in the west, from war bounties or from foresight and initiative, than any other man. Other estates were east of the fall-line or in the foothills of the Blue Ridge; Washington had taken five major journeys through the Potomac gap and into the fertile bottoms of the Ohio. He sensed a new world here of wealth and opportunity; he was seeking to have it "seated", in the Virginian phrase, and to make of the Tidewater a feeding and supplying area. He was in this sense both entrepreneur and frontiersman.

There is little evidence that this powerful Virginian interest was understood in Britain. Indeed, few enough of Washington's fellow-Virginians felt as strongly as he did, though some Scots governors, like Dinwiddie and Dunmore, and Scotch-Irish adventurers, like Croghan and Johnson, shared some of his dreams. The British policy towards the Indians indicated how little this land-hungry drive to the west was understood at home. Though the Line had gradually been pushed westward, it had been done by treaties between colonists and Indians, with the reluctant endorsement—or, in Hillsborough's day, the vehement opposition—of the Home Government. At the time of the passing of the Intolerable Acts, a royal proclamation raised the price of land east of the Line and reaffirmed it as a barrier. The extension of the southern boundary of the Province of Quebec and the administration of the fur trade from Canada nullified the claims of Virginians to land north and west of the Ohio. Just before he set off for the Second Continental Congress, Washington learnt that Governor Dunmore threatened to cancel the land patents issued under the Proclamation of 1754 on the ground that the surveyor was not qualified. These measures were not only irritating and confusing, they indicated a lack of sympathy with, and a faith in paper plans for, an area increasingly remote from the British connection, hard to control even by its own native sons, and looking not to the Atlantic but to the West.

Washington paid little heed to British efforts to restrain him because he knew better than the Governor how impossible it was for this "moving belt of human settlement", to use F. J. Turner's later phrase, to be curbed or thwarted. Washington's passion for land, perhaps the strongest of all his emotions, did not of course make him a democrat : he was never that. Nor has the frontier, though it has no doubt made for equality, gregariousness and materialism, necessarily restricted the opportunities for the emergence of influential, natural leaders and even natural aristocrats. Leadership on the frontier was concentrated in as few hands as in the Tidewater, perhaps fewer. Nor is it true to say that America's Manifest Destiny pointed West : few in the East cared much about it—Dunmore found that his war with the Shawnee in 1774 was little understood, and it is still, significantly, "Dunmore's War". What it is true to say is that Washington and a number like him—democrats and aristocrats, Scotch-Irish, Germans, French and native born—made the Destiny manifest by their enterprise and their vitality.

Land in the West, ownership of it unshared, a path outside the boundaries of maps drawn and edged in Whitehall; this and loyalty, too, made Washington a "patriot". From the moment the Associations were formed, Washington had identified himself with them. He did not want separation from Britain, but he was readier than most Virginians to recognise that it might come to that, and was unafraid of the consequences. His loyalty was simple and finite, like the man. He had not been abroad, except with Lawrence to the West Indies; had he been educated in the Lake District, like his brothers, or sent to sea as he had wished, no doubt his loyalty would have been directed to more distant symbols. But for Washington in 1775 self-interest, duty and what he came to regard as "right" pointed in the same direction. His identification with his "country" and his neighbours was the more complete because he was so little of an intellectual. His references to Mount Vernon—and they increase through the next eight years—are an indication of the grip his home and kindred had upon him. It was not unusual: this Roman feeling for the house and the red clay soil around it runs like a warm thread through the Virginian story. It was this same identification, though in his case more questioning, that moved Robert E. Lee to another fateful decision eighty-six years later. And when Lee made his decision, it was Washington whom he cited as exemplar. When again, as with Lee, the decision was made, there was no turning back. The days of resignations were over. Washington brought to the cause twenty-two years' experience in war and in affairs, a manner modest, dignified and disciplined, and the strength of purpose of a committed mind.

75

Chapter Five

Commander-in-Chief: Bunker Hill to Saratoga (1775–1777)

WASHINGTON'S commission as "General and Commander-in-Chief of the Army of the United Colonies" was dated 19th June 1775. He received it on the 20th and set out for Boston on the 21st, escorted from the city by a detachment of the Philadelphia Light Horse. His diary ceases for six years.

The Congress commissioned four Major-Generals and eight Brigadier-Generals (all but one New Englanders) to serve under him. The "first Major-General", Artemas Ward, was commanding the Massachusetts troops before Boston. Although he had seen service with Abercromby and was held in high regard in his own state, he was a politician rather than a soldier—"a fat old gentleman, who had been a popular church warden but had no acquaintance whatever with military affairs", was Charles Lee's typically unkind comment. On Washington's arrival in Cambridge, Ward loyally if uncordially surrendered the command to him.

The second Major-General was the enigmatic and eccentric Charles Lee. An English regular officer who had seen service in many countries and had been a General in the British Army, he was politically liberal but personally cynical and tactless, with a flair for languages that included an unhappy gift for sarcasm. Unhealthily lean, with "little manners, a great sloven, wretchedly profane", according to Dr. Belknap, he was always surrounded by dogs. "To say the truth," he said, "I think the strongest proof of a good heart is to love dogs and dislike mankind." His movements of the previous year suggest that he saw himself as the destined leader of the rebel cause. Congress gave him his position and his seniority on Washington's insistence, and Washington clearly regarded him as his principal assistant. "He is the first officer in military knowledge and experience in the whole army. . . . Zealously attached to the cause, honest and well meaning, but rather fickle and violent I fear in his temper."

Whatever doubts were to be cast on Lee's probity by his later intrigues and by his behaviour at Monmouth, his essay of 1774, *Strictures on a Pamphlet Entitled a "Friendly Address to All Reasonable Americans"*, in reply to Dr. Myles Cooper, was a remarkably shrewd and prophetic picture of the war. The British Army, he argued, was ineffective, recruited from the poorest classes, as short of generals as the American; the British would need to gain many victories before the colonies were subdued, whereas a single American victory could win the war; a simple form of training would transform the colonists into a formidable infantry; foreign aid was likely, for American trade would tempt the maritime powers of Europe. This analysis, from one with so much more experience than any native, reinforced Washington's belief that a short struggle, the defeat of the British Army in Boston and the conquest of Quebec, would bring the Ministry to terms. The strategy of Congress, and of Washington, discouraged guerrilla warfare and, rightly, discounted the Loyalists; a large and disciplined Continental Army was to bottle up the British, and "hover like an eagle over its prey, always ready to pounce it when the proper time comes". This gave hope of speedy victory, which might avert the danger of any more radical separation from Britain.

The two other Major-Generals, Philip Schuyler and Israel Putnam, were contrasting personalities; the former a wealthy Hudson Valley patroon, politically a moderate, serving as delegate at the Second Continental Congress from a state dangerously neutralist in attitude; the latter, square-jawed and peppery, the oldest but the most colourful of the generals, rough in manner and ill-educated, farmer and tavern-keeper, but experienced as a Connecticut scout in the French and Indian War and with a reputation for courage and dash that was a by-word in New England. A British agent heard a militia company in Massachusetts being exhorted to emulate Cæsar, Pompey and "Old Put", "and all such great men". Of the five senior generals named by Congress, only Putnam shared with Washington the distinction of unanimous election. A bigger tribute was paid him at Bunker Hill, when the mortally wounded Colonel Abercrombie requested that, if any rebels were to be hanged, his old comrade Putnam might be spared. His record in the war failed to justify his reputation.

Another appointment, also on Washington's recommendation, was of Horatio Gates as Adjutant-General, a post then akin rather to that of a Military Secretary. Gates was, like Lee, a British officer who had served in the colonies during the French and Indian War. He bought a farm in the Shenandoah Valley, "Traveller's Rest", and was not stirred to action until 1774. He had all Lee's knowledge of war but lacked his venom; he was kindly and sociable and attentive to the welfare of his men. When Washington set out for the North, he was accompanied by two other aides, young and handsome Philadelphians, Thomas Mifflin, soon to be Quarter-Master-General, and Joseph Reed, a personal secretary. They proved ready and skilful as speech writers, a talent in which the Commander-in-Chief was himself lacking. Washington confessed that he chose Mifflin "from a thorough persuasion of his integrity, my own experience of his activity, and finally because he stands unconnected with ... this, that or t'other man. . . . There is more in this than you can easily imagine."

On 25th June, Washington reached New York City and entered it in style, a purple sash over his blue uniform, a plumed hat on his head and nine volunteer companies assembled to do him honour. Here definite news reached him from Boston of the battle known, inaccurately, as Bunker Hill.

On the night of 16th–17th June, to anticipate a rumoured British move, a colonial force of some 1,200 men had set out to occupy Bunker Hill in Charlestown, commanding the port of Boston. By mistake they occupied the neighbouring Breed's Hill, and dug themselves in. Next day they were shelled from British ships, but they were not driven off until three frontal assaults had been made by British troops under William Howe. Even then they retired largely from a lack of ammunition. The American casualties were 449, of whom 145 were killed and missing; the British casualties were over 1,000, of whom 226 were killed. One-eighth of the British officers killed in the Revolutionary War fell on Breed's Hill, and almost half the British troops engaged were casualties. Well might Gage write to Lord Dartmouth, in giving an account of the battle, "the rebels are not the despicable rabble too many have supposed them to be, and I find it owing to a military spirit encouraged amongst them for a few years past, joined with an uncommon degree of zeal and enthusiasm".

Four hours after Washington entered New York City, Governor Tryon also entered it, after fourteen months' absence in Britain. He was not welcomed by the volunteers, but he was met by "his Majesty's well affected and loyal subjects", by the members of the Council, the judges of the Supreme Court, the Mayor, the clergy, and the governors of King's College (now Columbia University)—and by many trimmers who had welcomed the rebel commander in the afternoon.

Washington assured the Provincial Congress of New York that he was as much concerned with the re-establishment of peace and harmony with Britain as he was with "the fatal but necessary" operations of war. Leaving Schuyler to exercise discretion in the command in New York—"I do not wish to circumscribe you within narrow limits"—he moved on to Cambridge which he reached on 2nd July 1775.

The difficulties facing Washington on assuming command were formidable, and not the least of them was the impossibility of obtaining accurate information. He had no reliable facts about the population of the colonies, the number of volunteer companies, the supplies of firelocks, powder and cannon. Though distance from Britain gave time to prepare defences, there could be no hope of defeating her at sea without foreign aid, and until that aid came America's cities were vulnerable, for they were all seaports. There was no Continental military establishment and no staff. In 1775 there were probably no more than 200 gunsmiths in the American colonies, many of them in the Loyalist middle colonies. And Washington himself, though his service twenty years before had been active enough, had directed a regiment on a three-hundred-mile frontier, not an army on a continent covering 200,000 square miles; he admitted his "want of experience to move upon a large scale"; he knew little about strategy, even less about artillery, cavalry or medical administration.

His first "General Orders" (3rd July) called for "returns" of the troops around Boston and of their supplies of ammunition, and the first figures for the powder stores were extravagantly optimistic. It took him a week to discover that there were 16,600 enlisted men and N.C.O.s, of whom 9,000 were from Massachusetts—figures well below his expectations. The men, volunteers enlisted for short periods, were ill-equipped and ill-disciplined. Arms were of every age and type. When winter came on, Washington reported to Congress, the Army might be deemed "in a state of nakedness". Officers were casual and negligent, and some had been found guilty of cowardice at Bunker Hill. There was considerable jealousy over the seniority given by Congress, and the juniors were a mixed group, chosen mainly by election, and including small farmers and artisans, mechanics and innkeepers. Though the natural position of the Army was strong, some of the redoubts were badly sited. When Charles Lee described the difficulties, he might have been describing the situation in Virginia twenty years before.

"We found everything exactly the reverse of what had been represented. We were assured at Philadelphia that the army was stocked with engineers. We found not one. We were assured that we should find an expert train of artillery. They have not a single gunner and so on. So far from being prejudiced in favour of their own officers, they are extremely diffident in 'em and seem much pleased that we are arrived . . . The men are really very fine fellows, and had they fair-play would be made an invincible army."

Washington estimated the British strength at 10,000 to 12,000, well equipped and with good artillery; it was, in fact, 8,500, plus two battalions of marines and the strength of the fleet. This force could raid the coast, threaten Long Island Sound and raid Falmouth (now Portland, Maine), and Washington had to ignore appeals for help from the threatened ports. For it was in Boston that he expected the blow to fall and against that blow that he strove, from July to September, to organise the defences, and inspirit the officers and men. Though he agreed with Lee that the men might fight very well "if properly officered", he thought the New Englanders "an exceedingly dirty and nasty people". By the end of August he had, he said, "made a pretty good slam among such kind of officers as the Massachusetts government abound in . . . having broke one Colonel and two Captains for cowardly behaviour in the action on Bunker's Hill—two Captains for drawing more provisions and pay than they had men in their company—and one for being absent from his post when the enemy appeared there. . . ."

His efforts at discipline were not made any easier by the arrival in camp in late July of the riflemen recruited by Congress in June—nine companies from Pennsylvania, three more than were called for, and two each from Maryland and Virginia. Glad though Washington was to see them, especially Daniel Morgan's Virginians, who had marched 600 miles in twenty-one days, the "shirtmen" were hard to control. They were out to catch "lobsters" as they called the redcoats, and they appeared likely, by their fondness for sharpshooting, to use up the puny supply of powder and to encourage too many raids in retaliation. Nevertheless, their accurate fire and frontier training put fear into the British —"Never had the British Army so ungenerous an enemy," wrote William Carter; "they send their riflemen five or six at a time who conceal themselves behind trees, &c., till an opportunity presents itself of taking a shot at our advance sentries, which done they immediately retreat. What an unfair method of carrying on a war !"

Fair or otherwise, the appearance of the shirtmen from the South alongside the loosely-gathered New England companies of farmers and fishermen indicated that a continent not a city was in arms.

Of necessity, the initiative passed from the civilian and committee-ridden Congress to the army command; careful though Washington was to consult Congress and ready though he was to welcome the visits of the Congressional committees, most of the militants were with him in the field. "To you", Charles Lee told him, "they look up for decision; by your conduct they are to be inspired by decision. In fact, your situation is such that the salvation of the whole depends on your striking, at certain crises, vigorous strokes, without previously communicating your intention". His Council of War, consulted on the most important issues, consisted of three Congressional Major-generals, Ward, Lee and Putnam, and five Congressional Brigadiers, Thomas and Heath of Massachusetts, Spencer of Connecticut, Nathanael Greene of Rhode Island, whose military experience so far had been for six months as a private in a militia company, and John Sullivan of New Hampshire, an ambitious and eloquent Irishman, full of courage but devoid of luck. His force was grouped in three divisions, two brigades to a division; men became accustomed—though very reluctantly—to serving under general officers from colonies other than their own.

With an army now in the field, it was hard for Congress to pretend that its purposes were peaceful. On 11th August, Washington protested to Gage at the treatment he was showing captured officers, throwing "them indiscriminately into a common jail, appropriate for felons". Gage replied that only British mercy had led him to overlook "the criminal in the captive"; where officers were concerned, he acknowledged no rank "not derived from the King"; as to prisoners in general, their lives by the law of the land were "destined to the cord". In his reply to this, which ended the correspondence, Washington pointed out that thus far the King's friends in America had been "protected from the fury of a justly enraged people", but he went further in defending the rank of American officers. "The uncorrupted choice of a brave and free people was", he said, "the purest source and original fountain of all power". In justifying a military situation, he was led to endorse, if not to originate, a theory of popular sovereignty; independence was a reality eleven months before Jefferson and John Adams took up their pens.

Nor did it long remain a strategy of containment. Gage—soon replaced by William Howe, and recalled—was not apparently planning to attack the Americans. Writing to his brother on 10th September, Washington expressed his surprise—"I cannot devise what they are staying there for, nor why, as they affect to despise the Americans, they do not come forth, and put an end to the contest at once." In fact, Gage had written to Lord Dartmouth (24th July) saying that the only line of advance, by Boston Neck, was too narrow, and that his forces were too small to hold the town and at the same time to subdue the country. Bunker Hill, in fact, made him timid. Howe's caution, attributed by a popular song of the day ("The Battle of the Kegs") to his fondness for Mrs. Loring, the wife of his commissary ("Awake, awake, Sir Billy, there's forage on the plain, Ah! leave your little filly, and open the Campaign"), was due not only to strategy but to shortages, particularly of horses to pull his supply trains and guns if he were to attempt an offensive.

Washington, in September, proposed to his Council of War that they take the initiative and mount an attack on the city, but this was rejected, partly on military grounds, partly because they still hoped for a change of policy in London. "We are so well posted," wrote his secretary Joseph Reed, "provided with all necessities, and our troops so young".

By September other plans were being considered. When Congress hesitated about tackling Britain at sea, Washington acted on his own. Coastal vessels were armed and manned by soldiers bred to the sea—Glover's Essex County Regiment from Massachusetts. The *Hannah*, Captain Nicholson Broughton, and the *Lee*, Captain John Manley, and four others, were instructed to capture supplies without engaging British warships. The *Lee* captured the brig *Nancy* in November, and when Gates saw her papers he said he could not have made out a better invoice : small arms, musket shot, flints and a brass mortar weighing 2,700 lb. This was christened with a bottle of rum by Old Put when it reached Cambridge, and known as "Congress", but unlike its god-parent it exploded the first time it was fired.

The major offensive, however, was the plan to liberate Canada. It was believed to be lightly held—"The whole number of regulars in Canada", said Governor Trumbull of Connecticut, "does not exceed 700"; and it was thought ready, in Washington's phrase, "to run to the same goal" as the other United Colonies, "the only link wanting in the great continental chain of union". He prodded Schuyler to action in a letter of 20th August, and the New Yorker, along with Brigadier Richard Montgomery, undertook an offensive from Ticonderoga and Crown Point, taken so easily in May. They were to capture Fort St. John's, Fort Chambly and Montreal in succession, and then move down the St. Lawrence to Quebec. Schuyler, as addicted to caution as Trumbull was to optimism, said his force of 1,700 men would be too few to use against Quebec, after garrisoning his line of march; after all, there were Indians as well as

British to be faced. Washington undertook to dispatch a force of 1,000 or 1,200 to make a diversion, which would baffle the British commander in Canada, General Sir Guy Carleton. This force would proceed along a little-known route, through the forests of Maine, up the Kennebec River over the Dead River portages, and down the Chaudière, and would emerge on the St. Lawrence opposite Quebec. To command it Washington chose Benedict Arnold, a swarthy and quarrelsome, but bold and energetic, Massachusetts Colonel. Arnold, who had helped Allen to seize Ticonderoga but won little credit, had all the summer wished to attack Canada. With three companies of riflemen, one of them Morgan's Virginians, and a battalion of infantry, largely volunteers, with a wordy proclamation urging on the Canadians the value of an "indissoluble union", and with instructions to treat Catholic churches with particular respect, he was off in haste (17th September).

Montgomery's column advanced rapidly. Fort St. John's, however, with 500 men, held out for eight weeks before it fell on 3rd November. On 13th November Montreal was occupied without opposition, though General Carleton got away down-river to Quebec, disguised as a trapper.

Arnold's expedition, however, had been a saga of endurance over "the terrible carrying place" on the Maine–Canada divide. His men had been held together only by the will of Arnold and of Daniel Morgan—"whose appearance gave the idea history has left us of Belisarius". They lived on boiled candles and roasted moccasins until they reached the Chaudière. Colonel Enos, commanding the rear party, sent his supplies forward, but withdrew with his own men—to be court-martialled by Washington on his return to Cambridge. With his force reduced to 600 men, Arnold failed in an attempt to seize Quebec quickly, being repulsed by Colonel Allen Maclean and his Royal Highland Emigrants, and waited for Montgomery to come to the rescue with cannon, gunpowder and warm clothing.

When Montgomery did join him, however, their numbers were dwindling. The men, miserably clothed for a winter campaign, refused to overstay their dates of enlistment. Writing to Washington (22nd November 1775), Schuyler reported that 300 of Montgomery's men had marched away, too feeble to do military duty until given their discharge, when they "instantly acquired health" and set off on a 200-mile march home "with the greatest alacrity". "Nothing", he said, "can surpass the impatience of the troops from the New England colonies to get to their firesides".

On New Year's Eve Montgomery attempted a night attack through four-foot snowdrifts, but Carleton and Maclean had put heart into the defenders. Neither of the American feints was successful, and the snow rendered the rebel firelocks useless. Montgomery was killed, by the last shot fired by a drunken sailor; Arnold was carried off the field with a ball through his leg; Morgan and 370 others were made prisoners. The wrecked army was ravaged by a smallpox epidemic, that was "ten times more terrible than Britons, Canadians and Indians together", but it continued the siege through the long Canadian winter.

Smallpox was raging among the British and Loyalists in Boston, too. A British officer described the town as a scene of "melancholy, disease and death". "With regard to diet, we are obliged to live on salt beef and salt pork, much the greater part of which is hard as wood, as lean as carrion, and as rusty as the devil . . . our only beverage being new rum or spruce liquor, which soon throws us into the bloody flux, and runs us off our legs in a few days. . . . 'Tis well for our Generals that we have no where to run to. . . ." Relief ships were wrecked. Though Washington fumed at the inactivity and repeatedly proposed to his Council an attack on Boston —uniformly and unanimously rejected—his siege tactics were proving successful. This was not yet apparent, however, and criticism of Washington was mounting. He was fully aware of it. Writing to Congress, he said : "To have the eyes of the whole continent fixed with anxious expectation of hearing of some great event, and to be restrained in every military operation, for want of the necessary means of carrying it on, is not very pleasing, especially as the means, used to conceal my weakness from the enemy, conceals it also from our friends, and adds to their wonder".

Nor were his difficulties any less. His troops had been unwilling to serve beyond the date of enlistment, and the Connecticut Regiment had had to be brought back to Cambridge in December by force. Long furloughs had had to be given as a reward for re-enlistment. This pattern would prove recurrent; a year later Washington was still saying that, unless the people helped him in returning deserters, "we shall be obliged to detach one half of the army to bring back the other". There were shortages of tents, of wood, of powder, of clothing, of uniform—there never was to be consistency about uniform, and occasionally whole companies wore British scarlet, acquired from privateering ships—or by deserting to the British and re-deserting from them. Discipline improved slowly. Washington deplored the extent to which officers curried favour with their men—he found one Connecticut captain of horse shaving a private soldier on the parade near headquarters. He was convinced that sharp distinctions of rank were imperative : he wore a light blue riband across his breast, his generals pink, his aides green; officers were to wear cockades in their hats. Offences from card playing to "desertion" (absence without leave) were met by flogging—anything from 100 to 300 lashes, sometimes "to be well washed with salt and water after he has received his last fifty". In 1781 Washington was to recommend that courts-martial be allowed to increase the number of lashes to 500. Desertion in the modern sense was punishable by the death sentence. There were no illusions here and no sentimentality. He knew the "dirty mercenary spirit" of his troops, and dealt with it not by democratic exhortations or the "humanitarianism" of the Revolution, but by discipline. He knew, too, the military limitations of his men.

"Place them behind a parapet, a breast-work, stone wall, or anything that will afford them shelter, and from their knowledge of a firelock, they will give a good account of their enemy; but . . . they will not march boldly up to a work, nor stand exposed in a plain."

American skill at fortification and entrenchment was proved on 4th March when Washington seized Dorchester Heights, which commanded Boston and which made the city untenable under bombardment. The credit belongs as much to Ward and Heath, who had urged this for some time, and to Colonel Henry Knox, the Boston bookseller, who had brought over the mountains the cannon and mortars captured at Ticonderoga, as to the Commander-in-Chief. It was carried out smoothly, with the aid of a cannonade and with picked troops under Putnam waiting to attack the town if a sally were attempted by Howe. Howe, now Sir William, who had long been pointing out the superior strategic value of New York, withdrew his men from Boston on 17th March, and took with him to Halifax those Loyalists, a thousand in number, who could be carried. Washington informed Lee, who had moved to New York, of the likelihood that Howe's next move would be in that direction. And to Congress he reported his first success, the withdrawal of the enemy, and the supplies of cannon, coal, wheat and oats, powder and tools that he had won. He was publicly thanked, portraits and mezzotints and verse began to honour him, Harvard awarded him a Doctorate of Laws, and Congress ordered a gold medal struck in Paris. On one of the forts in Boston was the placard, "Welcome, Brother Jonathan".

The victory of March 1776 was not the end of a short-lived war—Washington's theory until now—but only of a campaign. Howe's withdrawal pointed to a long struggle, with the next blow directed at Halifax and the St. Lawrence, or at New York. Like the creation of the army, the waging of war was itself burning away the ties with Britain. The bloodshed, the embittered feelings of Patriots and Loyalists, the floggings, rumours of ill-treatment of American prisoners like Ethan Allen and reprisals against British, like the use of the abandoned mines at Simsbury, Connecticut, the burning of Norfolk by Dunmore, whom Washington described as "that arch-traitor to the rights of humanity"— all these were making further negotiation unlikely. In August 1775 the Americans had been declared rebels. In September, in Moscow, the Earl of Suffolk had made an attempt to hire 20,000 Russians; when that failed, mercenaries, mainly from Hesse-Kassel, were hired in Germany, and began to reach America in August 1776. In the end, there were to be 30,000 "Hessians". As Ambrose Serle, Lord Howe's Secretary, recognised, they "inflamed the Americans more than two or three British Armies . . . the dread, which the rebels have of these Hessians, is inconceivable : they almost run away at their name. Indeed, they spare nobody, but glean all away like an Army of Locusts". On a smaller scale altogether powder and arms began to reach the rebels from France and Holland. In November 1775, Lord North's Prohibitory Act established, on paper at least, a naval blockade of America. Although as late as January 1776, Pennsylvania and New York, New Jersey and Maryland, instructed their representatives still to vote against independence, the mood was uglier now.

And through the spring the doctrines of Tom Paine, expressed in *Common Sense* (January 1776), were reaching many Americans, decrying the inconsistency of protesting loyalty to a King while engaging in war against his Ministers. "Every thing that is right or reasonable pleads for separation. The blood of the slain, the weeping voice of nature cries, 'Tis Time to Part." Paine put the blame squarely and vehemently on the King, "the royal brute". *Common Sense* is the link between the Declaration of the Causes of Taking Up Arms of July 1775 and Jefferson's Declaration of Independence of July 1776. Massachusetts, North Carolina and Virginia had by May instructed their delegates to support or even to propose independence.

Common Sense moved even Washington, no theorist, to approval and endorsement—"sound doctrine and unanswerable reasoning". "I would tell them", he wrote Joseph Reed in February, "that if nothing else could satisfy a tyrant and his diabolical ministry, we are determined to shake off all connections with a state so unjust and unnatural. This I would tell them, not under covert but in words as clear as the sun in its meridian brightness." *Common Sense* expressed both the note of valour of a revolutionary cause and the note of victory, and by March 1776 Washington had experienced something of each. Although shortages of supplies and lack of pay, sectional rivalries, desertion and hardship and the awful risks of putting his men into battle would be with him through the next five years, there was implicit in the situation of 1776 a shred of hope. The British seemed to find movement into the interior difficult; their 3,000-mile-long line of communication was vulnerable; the North Carolina Loyalists had been overwhelmed at Moore's Creek Bridge; thanks to Charles Lee and Colonel William Moultrie, the attempted British landing at Charleston had failed; and at the top the British seemed to be as divided and as hesitant in counsel as the Americans. In his letter to Reed,

Washington said that he had favoured independence since October 1775. Certainly by March 1776 he had abandoned the pretence that all he was doing was bringing a reluctant pressure to bear on a hesitant Ministry to compel it into an unwilling compromise. He was now leading a rebellion against a tyrant, and step by step fathering the mythology of Independence.

If the evacuation of Boston ended the period of phoney war, it brought disasters in its train. Arnold's disease-ridden army in Canada was attacked in May by the reinforcements under Burgoyne that Lord George Germain, the new Colonial Secretary, sent to aid Carleton. Arnold lost cannon and ammunition, and was driven back in a "most precipitate and confused retreat". Washington recognised that the prospects of possessing Canada were now "almost over". Arnold retreated slowly southwards, contesting the Lake Champlain waterway. If the British could control this route, in 1776 as again in 1777, they could enter New York from the Hudson valley as well as from the sea, and isolate New England. Arnold improvised a naval force of galleys and gunboats—built in haste of green wood. He was outnumbered and beaten again at Valcour Island (October 1776) and his "navy" destroyed, but he had thwarted Carleton's efforts to join up with Howe in New York at least until 1777. Had he not done so, there would have been no surrender at Saratoga, and probably no French alliance. Moreover, his efforts had diverted British supplies and men from New York to the St. Lawrence. He had thus weakened Howe, delayed his attempt to regain control of the Middle States and had eased the pressure on Washington. Once again Arnold won no plaudits, except from Washington, for his skill and dash. First Thomas, then Gates, had been given command of the Northern forces. Arnold's accounts were in disorder, and for a time he was under arrest. His bitterness grew dangerously with his failure to win recognition.

Much more than Canada or Boston, the real strategic centre was New York, "the Grand Magazine of America", as Washington—and Howe—realised. The state was thinly populated, but the Hudson–Mohawk–Lake Champlain area was an overland route to Canada and to the Great Lakes; the city had the best harbour on the Atlantic coast, and seemed easily defensible by a fleet-supported army; it was, by and large, loyalist in its sentiments. This neutralism was more than a matter of mercantile caution, or of the deftness of the governor, William Tryon; the shore-line areas of Manhattan, Long Island and Staten Island were exposed to British warships. In January 1776, Charles Lee urged Washington to defend New York, with or without Congressional approval. "New York must be secured, but it never will . . . be secured by direct order of Congress. They find themselves awkwardly situated. . . ."

On 7th January, Washington sent Lee to Connecticut to recruit volunteers. With these he was to move into New York to prepare its defences and to disarm all "justly suspected" Tories. This alarmed Congress; it had just issued an order directing the individual colonies to disarm and arrest the more dangerous Tories, but requiring that any detachments of the army needed for this purpose should obey local civilian officials. New York Congressmen in particular, with the British ships riding at anchor in their harbour and more rumoured to be on the way, voiced what they euphemistically called their "prudent care" for their "lives and property". The militants in Congress supported Lee, and found the New Yorkers "timid and trimming to the greatest degree".

Although Lee behaved with discretion and had Washington's support, his difficulties indicated both the intricacies of the relationship between Congress and the Army, and the vulnerability of New York itself. Washington was much more civilian-minded than Lee—"I am not fond of stretching my powers"—and was in the end to profit from being so. And in fact the local situation was complex; even with a large and equipped force available, New York would be all but impossible to defend without sea-power. Lee told Congress that the city could be used only as a battle-ground. His own proposals for its defence by a camp on western Long Island proved quite futile against a major British invasion. That invasion came on 2nd July, when Howe brought a force of 32,000 men from Halifax and landed on Staten Island and, a month later, on Long Island itself.

But 2nd July was important for other reasons. Washington
and his army had arrived in New York in April. In May he
took counsel with Congress, and especially with Benjamin
Harrison, John Adams and R. H. Lee; with Gates and
Mifflin, he surveyed the defences of Philadelphia and the
Delaware River; he praised the Virginia resolves of 15th
May that Congress should declare the colonies free and independent states, at a time when, he noted to his brother,
"whole provinces are still feeding themselves upon the dainty
food of reconciliation". A permanent Board of War and
Ordnance was created, and Congress authorised three-year
enlistments. New plans were drawn up, for the use of 20,000
militia in Canada and New York, for the hiring of 2,000
Indians and for "flying camps" on the lines Charles Lee had
recommended for Virginia and the South, with which to
defend Pennsylvania and Maryland. Lee was in the South.
Gates was sent north—too late, as it proved—to take command in Canada.

Back in New York, Washington's presence, and that of
his army, gave new assurance to the patriots. He was given
an "elegant entertainment" by the New York Provincial
Congress, at which the thirty-one toasts included tributes to
"Mr. Burke . . . the protesting Lords" and "the late noble
Lord Howe", whose brother, the new Lord, was then leading the British fleet towards Staten Island. Communication
with British ships was cut off. Gouverneur Morris and his
secret committee of the New York Congress disclosed to
Washington the "Tory Plot", whereby Tryon, from his
headquarters on the warship *Duchess of Gordon*, and the
royalist Mayor David Matthews, were recruiting men for
service in the British Army; they were to rise in the city in
conjunction with the forthcoming attack of the main British
Army. There were rumours that the plot included an
attempt on Washington's life. The Mayor was arrested at
Flatbush—though not as yet for engaging in "treason",
since formal independence had not yet been proclaimed. His
crime, in fact, was simply allegiance to an authority now
rejected by his more militant fellow-countrymen. But if
not a civil crime, such treachery committed by a member of
the Continental Army was punishable by death. Thomas

Hickey, of Washington's bodyguard, was hanged, the first revolutionary soldier to pay the price of treason.

On 24th June, Congress resolved this dilemma by passing the Allegiance and Treason Resolves defining the King as an enemy. R. H. Lee had introduced in Congress on 7th June his resolution that "these United Colonies are, and of right ought to be, free and independent States". It was a matter of right, no doubt, but it was also a matter of strategy; local —to bring pressure on hesitant states; and international—to win foreign aid. "It is not choice . . . but necessity that calls for independence," R. H. Lee wrote, "as the only means by which foreign alliances can be obtained." On 2nd July, Congress approved Lee's resolution, and two days later adopted Jefferson's draft of a Declaration of Independence. It listened also to the reading of a letter from Washington, dated 30th June :

"When I had the honor of addressing you yesterday, I had only been informed of the arrival of forty-five of the [British] fleet in the morning. Since that time I have received authentic intelligence . . . that one hundred and ten sail came in before night that were counted, and that more were seen about dusk in the offing. I have no doubt but that the whole that sailed from Halifax are now at the Hook."

The brothers Howe, General Sir William and Admiral Lord Richard, brought to New York the largest expeditionary force of the eighteenth century, 34,000 men, many of them Germans. Washington had no more than 20,000, ill-trained and ill-equipped, many of them militia who had never smelled gunpowder. On 27th August Howe attacked and outflanked Putnam, who was holding a wooded ridge south of the fortifications guarding the East River. The American losses were 1,500, the British 300. Washington hurried six regiments over the East River into the Brooklyn entrenchments, and had Howe struck again quickly they would probably all have been lost. Realising his peril, Washington drew his forces back to Manhattan Island, and was fortunate that rain and fog gave him cover and respite.

Here he was equally vulnerable to the same tactics. The invaders had control of the sea lanes, though they used them hesitantly; they were skilful at flanking movements and had

ample information of the local situation from Tory sympathisers. The situation indeed was gloomy; whole regiments of militia were leaving the sinking cause—"as prac-
ticable to stop a torrent, as these people when there time is
up". There was little faith in Washington. "Would to
Heaven General Lee were here is the language of officers
and men", wrote one of the Delaware Continentals. Lee,
wrote another, is hourly expected from Charleston, but "as
if from heaven, with a legion of flaming swordsmen". The
Howes, in their capacity as peace commissioners, offered
negotiation, but their offer was rejected when it was clear
that it called for complete surrender.

The British landings in mid-September at Kip's Bay
(now the foot of 34th Street), preceded by a naval bombardment, were practically unopposed, and Washington fell back
to Harlem Heights (at approximately 125th Street). While
he was here, part of the city was burned—for which New
Yorkers blamed equally the British, the Hessians and New
Englanders—and Nathan Hale was caught by Howe's
troops, and executed as a spy. On 12th October Howe
moved by water up the East River to New Rochelle, by-
passing again and threatening to pin the Continentals
against the Hudson. Leaving Greene with 5,000 men to
guard Fort Washington (close to the present George Washington Memorial Bridge) and Fort Lee (on the Jersey
Shore) and thus control the Hudson, Washington drew back
to White Plains (October). Here he was attacked by superior
forces, now including some cavalry to which his men were
unaccustomed, and he pulled farther back across the Croton
River.

Worried now about his forts and by a possible invasion of
New Jersey, Washington left Lee (5,000 men) and Heath
(3,000 men) on the eastern shore of the Hudson to hamper
any British drive up the Hudson Valley or into New England, and crossed the river at Peekskill with his "main"
force. He reached Fort Lee on 13th November. He had advised Greene to withdraw from Fort Washington, but left
the final decision to his discretion. While they debated,
Howe overran the fort (16th November 1776), capturing
2,800 Americans, their equipment and their guns. "I feel
mad, vexed, sick and sorry," wrote Greene to Knox. "Never

did I need the consoling voice of a friend more than now."
It was Greene's sole error of judgment in the whole war;
had Howe's troops struck half an hour earlier, they would
have captured both Greene and Washington.

With unusual speed, Howe followed up this success by
sending Cornwallis with 5,000 men across the river. As
Washington's dwindling and dispirited force retreated towards Newark, Cornwallis' troops scaled the solid rock of
the Palisades and took Fort Lee. Charles Lee, playing his
own hand, responded slowly to Washington's orders to
come to his support in New Jersey, and was captured by a
British scouting party in December. This was deemed the
heaviest blow of all.

With a force now of less than 5,000, there was nothing
for the Commander-in-Chief to do but retreat across New
Jersey, "from its levelness and openess, unfit for making a
stand", across the Delaware and into Pennsylvania (8th
December). The British plan of campaign called for Howe
to advance up the Hudson and aid in crushing Arnold, but
Howe was a cautious and conventional soldier and the
season was late; it was time for winter quarters, and after
the triumphs, the comforts and alleviations of war, time to
exchange the helmet for a nightcap. He gave orders to
Cornwallis to chase Washington beyond New Brunswick,
and to find winter quarters for his troops in eastern New
Jersey.

It was an ignominious story; a series of routs, with Washington at Kip's Bay beating his troops with his cane and
half-demented in his efforts to make them stand their
ground. The retreat he described himself as "disgraceful
and dastardly". The British had taken New York and controlled most of New Jersey in less than three months' cam-
paigning, and with few casualties; New York remained in
their hands throughout the war. Washington had committed
his troops to the defence of New York City at the behest of
Congress, in full knowledge of the risks imposed by its
insular character. For this reason, he had rejected the forth-
right advice of Henry Knox, Nathanael Greene and Joseph
Reed, now Adjutant-General, that the city be evacuated and
burned. It would not help the morale of the cause, at home
or abroad, if the Americans abandoned so important an

area without a fight. The rumour that the city was to be destroyed and abandoned had caused a panic, and Washington had given the assurance that "nothing but the last Necessity" would warrant it. When he laid the problem before Congress (2nd September 1776), Congress forbade its destruction.

The repeated division of his forces had proved unwise, yet the purpose behind it—the maintenance of control over the Hudson—could not be faulted. Washington was correct enough in trying to control the river; it was on its upper reaches in the following year that there came the turning-point of the war. Nevertheless, his hesitations at Brooklyn Heights and at Fort Lee had proved costly. His orders to both Lee and Greene, though clear enough, had not been sufficiently peremptory. His tactical positions were often exposed and vulnerable. He had critics in Congress, Richard Henry Lee among them, critics among his fellow-generals, like Gates and Charles Lee, critics even on his own headquarters staff. His secretary, Reed, and General Charles Lee, in a correspondence Washington came upon by accident, joined in deploring "an indecisive Mind".

The outlook in December was vastly different from that in March. Congress reasoned that when the Delaware River froze, Philadelphia, too, would fall to the British, and it prudently moved to Baltimore, giving Washington full powers to act. The British swarmed across New Jersey to Trenton and Bordentown—and garrisoned them, with unfortunate political results, with German troops. Howe offered pardons to all who would submit, and 3,000 accepted. The American cause looked hopeless; Washington's numbers now were down to 3,000 and more would leave on 1st January. Flour was lacking, clothing was lacking, pay was lacking. He wrote in despair to one brother, "I am wearied almost to death"; all he sought was "the peaceable enjoyment" of his "own vine and fig-tree", now farther away than ever; and a little later to another, "I think the game is pretty near up". Tom Paine's pamphlet *The Crisis*, written during the retreat, began with the words :

"These are the times that try men's souls. The summer soldier and the sunshine patriot will, in this crisis, shrink from the service of their country; but he that stands it *now* deserves the love and thanks of man and woman."

Paine also recognised in Washington "a natural firmness . . . which cannot be unlocked by trifles". Lee's troops, now commanded by Sullivan, reached Washington on 20th December; Mifflin induced 1,500 Pennsylvania militia to join him; Schuyler sent 1,000 men under Gates from the North. In this moment, when his fortunes were at the lowest, Washington resolved on a bold stroke. The nearest enemy detachment was a body of Hessians at Trenton, commanded by Colonel Rall. If the men could be judged by their commander's habits, they would hold high revel at Christmas. The night was cold and bleak, with snow and a piercing wind, the river a torrent of jagged blocks of ice. Nevertheless, with 2,400 men, Washington crossed the Delaware on Christmas night. It seems unlikely that his face bore the look of brooding calm that Leutze's romanticised portrait gave it seventy years later—with the Rhine replacing the Delaware as background. His two supporting columns failed to cross, but his attack on Trenton caught Rall completely —and personally—unprepared, despite Loyalist warnings of imminent attack. The Hessian commander, still fuddled from the night's celebrations, fell mortally wounded, and 1,000 of his men were captured. Tradition has it that two of Washington's men were frozen to death on the march; there were few losses in the action itself, though a future President, James Monroe, had a shoulder wound. As the other British units in western New Jersey retreated, Washington recrossed the river to rest his troops. The engagement was as courageous as it was successful, and it restored American morale. Congress, "having perfect reliance in the wisdom, vigour and uprightness of General Washington", gave him complete military powers for six months. He made full use of his powers to induce his soldiers to stay on, he pledged his own private fortune to pay them, he begged for "hard Money" from Robert Morris, and got 50,000 dollars. By 2nd January he had about 5,000 men.

The British were as alarmed as the Americans were elated by the *coup* at Trenton—"All our hopes were blasted," said Lord George Germain, the British Secretary of State, "by the unhappy affair." "The people", wrote the British traveller Nicholas Cresswell, "are all liberty-mad again. Confound the turncoat scoundrels and the cowardly Hessians together. . . . D—— them all." Cornwallis, with 8,000 men, moved out to meet Washington, and left garrisons at Princeton and Maidenhead. Washington moved to Trenton, and took up position on the Assunpink River. "At last we have run down the old fox," said Cornwallis, "and we will bag him in the morning."

But in the morning he was not there, and Cornwallis was awakened by the sound of cannon at Princeton; while his camp-fires burned through the night, Washington had moved his army, circled the enemy, and surprised and defeated the three British regiments there. Cornwallis, his line of supply cut and this mobile force prowling in his rear, prudently withdrew, and Howe pulled his detachments closer to New York. When Washington went into winter quarters in the hills around Morristown, he had in three weeks largely undone Howe's campaign of six months. He had regained the greater part of the Jerseys, in face of an enemy force better disciplined and infinitely more numerous than his own. Washington's name, wrote Cresswell, "is extolled to the clouds". By keeping Howe's attention focused on New Jersey and Philadelphia, Trenton was to prove as decisive an event as Saratoga.

This brief campaign is one of the few glimpses the war affords of Washington as a tactical commander; so much of his attention was devoted to the endless round of administration, the complaints and the politics of war. Brief enlistments, illness and desertion kept his numbers down. He was still scornful of the militia, "this mixed, motley crew, here to-day, gone to-morrow", though, both in New Jersey and New York, they rallied to him whenever he was successful. What Washington wanted was a professional army, "the Continental Line", and in September Congress agreed that eighty-eight battalions be enlisted "for the duration of the war", with bounties in money and in land. In November, however, it changed its mind and solicited only three-year terms. In any case, this was a paper plan only; states like Massachusetts and Connecticut were undermining the national effort by offering higher bounties for service at home in the militia—and good money, too, rather than suspect Continental paper. As in Cambridge, Washington wanted a united effort and a united country :

"I have laboured, ever since I have been in the service, to discourage all kinds of local attachments and distinctions of country, denominating the whole by the greater name of *American*, but I have found it impossible to overcome prejudices. . . ."

His forces were half-starved and half-clothed. Many of his men in the Trenton battle were barefoot, and the line of their march was visible in the blood that scarred the snow. One result of the Old Colonial System was now evident, the lack of American woollens, and the supplying of uniforms— when there were any—made of linen only. He was negotiating over prisoners, and complaining of the "infamous mercenary ravages" of the Hessians. He was worried, as always, over discipline : company politics that led officers to protect their men, lashings that were treated rather as sport than punishment, thieving and drunkenness—"the Barrel Fever". He was worried, too, about medical conditions, and not least about smallpox, which threatened to devastate his force as it had done Arnold's. There was considerable opposition to inoculation, then carried out not with the vaccine but with the human virus. Washington persuaded Martha to be inoculated while they were in Philadelphia together, and in New York carried out tests which proved that it killed only four men out of 500. In the early spring of 1777 the Morristown churches became hospitals to house an army of inoculated men.

Martha joined her husband in March, along with Lucy Knox and "Lady" Stirling, at Colonel Jacob Arnold's tavern, his headquarters. She presided over his table, from which, John Adams noted approvingly, wine had been banished. Occasionally Washington was able "to throw off the hero", wrote Mrs. Bland to her sister. "He can be downright impudent sometimes—such impudence, Fanny, as you and I like. . . ."

The campaign of 1777–8 was marked by a success, a failure, an ordeal and a conspiracy. The success was Gates', at Saratoga; the failure and the ordeal were Washington's; and the conspiracy was an attempt to supplant him.

It has long been assumed that the British plan for 1777, like that for 1776, looked to the permanent conquest of the Hudson Valley, just as it has also been assumed that it was Lord George Germain's slackness with dispatches in London that wrecked it. There is no evidence for either of these views. There was little, perhaps too little, direction of the war from "Whitehall"; Germain, a meticulous organiser, nevertheless believed in giving the "man on the spot" considerable latitude. The British plan in the 1777 campaign was Burgoyne's and Carleton's and Howe's, not Germain's. Carleton wanted to complete in 1777 what he had almost succeeded in doing the year before, to free Canada from the threat of American invasion, to reinforce Howe by land— to do so by sea would leave Canada exposed, and the anxious wait for Burgoyne's reinforcements in 1776 was too recent a memory—and, by compelling Washington to divide up his puny army still further, to facilitate Howe's own movements.

The planning was Carleton's, but Germain disliked him, so the command went to Burgoyne, who had spent the winter 1776-7 in London, persuading Germain of the merits of the plan and of his own qualities as a leader. It is true that Germain gave no orders to Howe to assist Burgoyne—a point on which the Whigs seized in order to attack the Ministry; nor did he inform Burgoyne of Howe's own plans (Howe did so himself). Howe, naturally deceived by the speed of his success in New York and New Jersey, favoured the invasion of Pennsylvania, where the Tories would rally to him; a small force on the lower Hudson would be enough to help Burgoyne. Germain shared this optimism; Philadelphia could be taken quickly, and Howe could then, if necessary, march back north to co-operate with Burgoyne. The two campaigns appeared fully compatible; only Clinton thought it, or said later that he thought it, a gamble.

By 1st July 1777, Burgoyne had reached Ticonderoga. He had 7,000 men, almost half of whom were Germans, and ample artillery, but he never had adequate transport. The Americans (2,300 men) evacuated the fort without a fight and retreated to the junction of the Mohawk and the Hudson. Here Burgoyne was to have been met by a diversionary force of 1,600 British and Iroquois Indians under Colonel Barry St. Leger and the Mohawk chief Brant, moving down the St. Lawrence to Oswego and then along the Mohawk. This column, however, while besieging Fort Stanwix, was checked at Oriskany by a band of frontier Germans under General Herkimer, and when a second American army under Arnold approached, St. Leger retreated to Oswego and Montreal; his Indian allies deserted what seemed to be the losing cause, and Burgoyne was left to fend for himself.

Burgoyne spent a month collecting supplies. He sent two large foraging parties into Vermont, but they were attacked at Bennington by John Stark and the Green Mountain Boys, and all 1,000 of them were killed or captured. These successes brought the New England militia, almost as volatile in their allegiance as the Indians, to Gates' colours; in the end, he had 12,000 militia and 5,000 Continentals. Burgoyne had 6,000 mouths to feed, an army overloaded with baggage and with wives, and his transport was wearing out. Congress did not help the American cause by shuffling the command between Gates and Schuyler—there were five changes of command between the two in fifteen months. Gates was, in October 1777, the chosen of Congress and the chosen of Fortune. Whether or not he personally deserved the victory, he won the confidence of the Yankee militia, as Schuyler did not; he had able subordinates, Morgan of Virginia, with his riflemen, sent to his aid by Washington, Benjamin Lincoln of Massachusetts, and Arnold, brash and as jealous as ever; and he disposed his forces ably in strongly entrenched positions at Saratoga.

Burgoyne attempted twice to cut through, unsuccessfully (19th September, 7th October). Only a quick retreat could have saved his army, and this he did not attempt, in the hope that Clinton might arrive from the South to his aid. The Baroness von Riedesel, wife of the commander of the Brunswick troops with Burgoyne, has left in her *Memoirs* a vivid description of the plight of the dwindling, stranded and hungry army, and a vividly hostile description of its chief, spending half the nights singing and drinking, "and amusing himself with the wife of a commissary, who was his mistress, and who, as well as he, loved champagne". On

14th October, twenty miles away from his target, Albany, he offered to negotiate, and the "Convention of Saratoga" was signed on the 17th.

Saratoga was not a total disaster, and it was, nominally at least, a convention not a surrender. A band played "Yankee Doodle", and toasts were drunk to King George and to General Washington. The Anglo-German troops, now 5,000, were to abandon arms and material, march to Boston, and embark on British transports on condition that they did not again serve in America. These were easy terms won from Gates by "Gentleman Johnny," the skilful playwright, when his soldierly qualities had failed him; but it was the arms that Gates wanted, for Clinton was pushing north, and Gates' own militia were leaving him already. The "Convention Army", as it came to be known, did not, however, reach Britain until after the war. Congress found a series of excuses to reject Gates' terms, and the Army was shuttled back and forth between Virginia and Massachusetts, presenting "the first prisoner and internment problem in American history". When they finally sailed for Europe in 1783, 1,500 chose to stay behind.[1]

Nevertheless, Saratoga transformed the war. A large British army had been destroyed; the Americans had again decisively denied the Hudson Valley to the British; and, in particular, the victory made France an active ally. For two years, through Beaumarchais and his fictitious company, Hortalez et Compagnie, trading nominally with the West Indies, supplies had been reaching America secretly and illicitly. The weapons of the American forces at Saratoga had been largely supplied by France. Sympathetic though it was, not even Benjamin Franklin's synthetic popularity could induce the French court to declare war until there was evidence of a chance of American victory. That was provided —or held to be provided—by Saratoga. In fact, it was less victory in the field that turned the tide than Vergennes' fears of the British conciliation proposals, on which Franklin and Beaumarchais played. These proposals, presented by North to Parliament in November 1777, hung fire over the

[1] See William Dabney's account of their experiences: *After Saratoga: the Story of the Convention Army* (University of New Mexico Press, Albuquerque, 1954).

Christmas season, and were not approved until 17th February 1778. It was too late then. On 6th February 1778, political and commercial treaties were signed by which France recognised the independence of the revolting colonies and agreed to make war upon Britain until American independence was won. Neither side was to make a separate peace without the consent of the other.

In April 1779, Spain came in as an ally of France—though not an ally of America—and for her own good reasons—to regain Gibraltar and the Floridas. The Dutch gave financial aid to the American cause, and by 1780 were at war with Britain over questions of neutral rights at sea. Britain faced also the League of Armed Neutrality, which by 1783 all the major and many of the minor states of Europe had joined. Britain's political and trading rivals in Europe were using the situation to their advantage; the colonial war had become world wide. America by her treaties had become entangled in the affairs of Europe—in ways so embarrassing that she deplored entangling alliances for the next 170 years; and Britain, facing again her European foes, began to consider the independence of America a price that it might be cheap to pay. With France in the field, the American war, as again in 1812, became a side-show.

The character of the struggle in America was thus transformed. French and Spanish and Dutch money and ships of war came to American aid, and "volunteers", too, from all over Europe : the young Lafayette, enthusiastic, lovable and ambitious for "glory"; Berthier, later one of Napoleon's Marshals; the Baron de Kalb, whose original mission was to persuade Congress to replace Washington as Commander by his patron, the Comte de Broglie; the Pole Pulaski, who, like de Kalb, was to die serving America; Kosciusko who organised the defences of Saratoga and West Point and was to Gates what Lafayette was to Washington, aide and admirer; and that Prussian drill-captain von Steuben, whose rank Franklin inflated to that of General, and who drilled Washington's men at Valley Forge. The aid was welcome, the men, the ships and the money. Not only welcome but timely, for there was no jingoism left in Washington's army in the winter of 1777. Indeed, by February 1778 there was hardly an army left at all.

Chapter Six

Commander-in-Chief: Valley Forge to Victory (1777—1783)

WHILE Gates' fortunes were in the ascendant, Washington's were at their lowest ebb. He faced a season of defeat, hardship and intrigue.

Howe, who by going north might have made Saratoga a British instead of an American victory, chose to invade Pennsylvania and to compel Washington to do battle to defend Philadelphia; a double blow, in the North and in the Middle States, would, he believed, end the war. In the spring, Howe undertook a series of reconnaissances from New York, in which his Hessians were checked at Brunswick by Morgan's riflemen and by a brigade under Anthony Wayne. In July he abandoned the overland campaign, put his troops on his brother's transports and sailed for the Chesapeake with an armada of 260 ships and 15,000 men. This move baffled Washington, who felt sure the goal was to be the Hudson. When the fleet appeared off Delaware Bay, he moved to Wilmington. When it sailed on, he thought its destination Charleston. He was "compeld to wander about the country like the Arabs in search of corn". When the news of Howe's real destination reached him (22nd August), he had just sent north to oppose Burgoyne all the troops he could spare, including the leaders, Morgan, Lincoln and Arnold, who did so much to win the day at Saratoga.

To defend Philadelphia, Washington took a stand on the Brandywine creek (11th September) with 8,000 Continentals and 3,000 militia. Again he was outflanked. The British forces, especially Cornwallis', were skilfully handled and their movements precisely timed. The Americans paid the price of ignorance of ground and of faulty and conflicting intelligence. The country was Quaker, the people, said

Washington, "to a man disaffected"; "a breed of mongrels", said Adams. But the army, though defeated, retreated in good order, with its artillery still intact.

After falling back over the Schuylkill River, Washington recrossed (15th September) with a force in which 1,000 were barefoot, to risk a battle at White House Tavern in a vulnerable position. He was rescued by a heavy rainstorm, which drenched the powder of both armies. He left 1,500 men under Wayne near Paoli, Pennsylvania, to threaten Howe's rear; a British detachment attacked this force at night, their campfires making of their silhouettes easy targets for a bayonet charge, and inflicted 300 casualties without firing a shot. But Philadelphia was conceded two days before the "Paoli Massacre", when Colonel Alexander Hamilton, Washington's aide, urged Congress to leave. Howe's advance units entered the city on 27th September.

Howe split his army, and the Germantown section was daringly attacked by Washington (4th October), suffering heavy losses. The defence of the Chew House prevented an American victory, and reinforcements from Philadelphia finally drove Washington off, but, according to Arthur Lee in Paris, this engagement impressed Vergennes as much as did Saratoga. Howe then settled down to winter in the discreetly friendly city; his troops were warm, well-fed and loyally done by, and even his Hessians found sympathisers among the German-speaking Pennsylvanians. Washington took his men into quarters at Valley Forge, twenty miles outside Philadelphia, on the banks of the Schuylkill. For him it was the winter of his discontent, the midnight of the Revolution.

Valley Forge : though set in the midst of a rich and fertile farming country, it was in fact a bleak plateau, and the farms for miles around had been swept bare of grain and cattle in the preceding campaign. It was, said Washington, "a dreary kind of place, and uncomfortably provided". His men lived in shabby tents until they felled the trees to make logs for cabins—but there were few nails or tools for building them. Half of them were without blankets, nearly half without shoes. "All my men," reported Colonel Livingston, "except eighteen are unfit for duty for want of shoes, stockings and shirts, breeches and coats . . . and . . . we are becoming ex-

ceedingly lousy." Sullivan reported his officers "so naked they
were ashamed to be seen". Even the deserters could hardly
leave camp for lack of decent covering. While the British ate
good beef and butter from rich Pennsylvania "Dutch" lar-
ders, the Americans drank soup "full of burnt leaves and dirt,
enough to make a Hector spew". "Poor food—hard lodging
—cold weather—fatigue—nasty clothes—nasty cookery—
vomit half my time—smoked out of my senses—the Devil's
in't—I can't endure it," wrote the surgeon Albigence Waldo.

But they did endure; they grew as tough and determined
as they were lean, and after Steuben's arrival they were better
drilled than ever before. Washington's greatest achievement
as commander was to keep an army in being and to train it at
Valley Forge. He always declared afterwards that Howe
could still have won the war had he attacked at that point;
so long as he endured, he prevented the British dominating
the central colonies, and threatened them both in New York
and Philadelphia.

In April came the news of the replacement of the slow-
moving Howe by the even more slow-moving Clinton, of the
British "peace offensive", offering Home Rule and a negotiated peace; and of the treaty with France, offering Independence through victory. The winter was over. The Army
celebrated by a salute of thirteen cannon, and every man had
a gill of rum. Washington's officers presented a play, one of
the General's favourites, Addison's *Cato*; it must have stirred
memories of Virginia and of Sally Fairfax, now a Loyalist in
England.

The months at Valley Forge saw the testing not only of an
army but of its commander. With Philadelphia fallen and
Congress chased out for a second time, with France not yet
in the war, and with the Continental Army few in numbers
and poor in discipline, criticism of Washington reached its
peak. The long struggle was producing strains and tensions
among both officers and Congressmen.

There was always in Congress a laudable democratic
undercurrent of fear of military leadership. Though in crises
Washington had been given wide powers and though by
temperament he would be the last to abuse them, Congress
believed in the principle of civilian control. It had checked

him at first by using visiting Committees of Congressmen, and then by setting up a creaky Board of War; it had opposed the proposals for a standing army. Still in large measure a gathering of diplomats from individual states, it had wrangled long over promotions. John Adams had once even suggested that the General officers should be annually elected.

In the two years since 1775, the membership of Congress had changed considerably; only six remained of those who had originally enthused over Washington's appointment. There was increasing criticism of the hero-worship, and of what seemed at times the sycophancy of his aides. By 1777 Washington's "family", as he called it, was a group of devotees; Stirling and Sullivan and Morgan of the field officers, Tench Tilghman and Alexander Hamilton, Greene and Knox and Lafayette of the staff. As early as February 1777, John Adams was deploring "the superstitious veneration that is sometimes paid to General Washington", and he rebuked those members of Congress "disposed to idolise an image which their own hands have molden". In October, he wrote to Abigail—"Now we can allow a certain citizen to be wise, virtuous and good, without thinking him a deity or a savior."

A further source of trouble was the Northern reaction to some of Washington's remarks about Yankees, no more pungent than those about his fellow-Southerners, but at once offending. One reason for his selection had been to offset sectionalism, and the few occasions when he seemed to show some sectional prejudice were humanly resented. It was again John Adams, even more sensitive than Washington, who protested to Henry Knox—"Pray, tell me, Colonel Knox, does every man to the southward of Hudson's River behave like a hero, and every man to the northward of it like a poltroon, or not? . . ."

The core of the criticism of 1777 was simply that Washington had failed to defeat Howe, while Gates had won renown for the success at Saratoga. Washington was thought of, far from accurately, as a Fabius, and the term was not meant in flattery. "Our affairs are Fabiused into a very disagreeable position," wrote Congressman Lovell. His keenness, not shared by his Generals, to attack Howe in Boston and in Philadelphia; his near-recklessness at Trenton, where it succeeded, and at Germantown, where it just missed success;

this belligerence—emerging particularly when things looked blackest—was disregarded, as it has been disregarded by so many of his later biographers.

From the beginning Washington had taken the decision that the war must be defensive, a war of posts—"We should on all occasions avoid a general action, nor put anything to the risk unless compelled by a necessity into which we ought never to be drawn." This strategy was abundantly sound, in terms of American forests and hills, and was made even more so by the British hesitations to risk a general engagement; but it was not to Washington's liking. His own instinct was for action, for attack. And his apparent inactivity provoked a natural criticism in Congress. It came mainly from John Adams, from Benjamin Rush, who spoke scornfully to Gates about the "incense-burning" at Washington's headquarters, from James Lovell of Massachusetts, from Richard Henry Lee of Virginia and from the former Quarter-master, Thomas Mifflin of Pennsylvania, who had broken with the Commander-in-Chief because he had not, he thought, moved quickly enough to defend the Middle States.

This criticism was brought into the open with the discovery of a private letter to Gates, written by a Major-General Thomas Conway (an Irish-born French officer serving on leave with the Continentals), expressing the hope that Gates might replace the "weak General". This letter was revealed to Stirling (and by him to Washington) by a drunken aide of Gates, James Wilkinson. Wilkinson's intrigues in the revolutionary war, like his later role in the Burr Conspiracy, make him an unreliable witness, but there is no doubt of the tenor of the correspondence. When Conway, having admitted his criticism, went farther, and defended the right of free expression of opinion in a free country, even though of Commanders by Major-Generals in the middle of a war, and then apologised for it because he had not the "prodigious height" of the "great Frederick" or the "great Washington", the Commander-in-Chief had had enough. The correspondence was laid before Congress (January 1778). Conway offered his resignation and was mortified at its prompt acceptance; he was challenged and badly wounded in a duel —with pistols at ten paces—with General John Cadwalader, and returned to France.

Was there, however, a "Conway Cabal", an organised group plotting to replace Washington by Gates? Washington and his aides certainly believed in the existence of a "malignant faction", but there is no real evidence to support it.[1] Criticism is one thing, conspiracy another. Reed and Charles Lee, Kalb and Mifflin, had all been critical of Washington's strategy without necessarily involving Congress. The issue really turned not on Conway but on Gates, and on his New England supporters in Congress. Gates had certainly cultivated Congressmen, before and after Saratoga; he had reported the news of Saratoga direct to Congress, not to his Commander-in-Chief, and was gently rebuked for it; he had become President of the Board of War, with ill-defined, semi-political powers of inspection; and he had his own military following. But so had Washington, and so indeed has every able commander; one of the first marks of successful leadership in war is the ability to recruit dedicated staff officers. Gates was a shrewd organiser, popular with the troops, and his replacement of Schuyler in the Hudson Valley—even if to some degree a Congressional intrigue—had been a sound move. Nor does advocacy by more than one person of a change of command necessarily imply a concerted plan; frequent changes of command, especially after failure, are normal military practice. The charge that there was a Cabal must remain non-proven.

The failure of the "conspiracy" in fact immensely strengthened Washington. Conway was broken, and with him went not only a "dangerous incendiary", but a "foreigner". Washington's headquarters swarmed with Frenchmen—there was, reported Silas Deane in Paris, a "rage" for America among French officers—and, however valuable the services some of them rendered, especially Pulaski in the belated organisation of cavalry, Du Portail as an engineer and Steuben as a drill-master, they were, for Washington, another cross to bear. They were all, in one degree or another, *condottieri*, serving first their own careers. They came with contracts signed in Paris by Silas Deane or Franklin, often

[1] The two most recent studies, Bernhard Knollenberg, *Washington and the Revolution* (1941) and L. H. Butterfield's edition of *The Letters of Benjamin Rush* (1951), offer convincing denials of the existence of any cabal.

promising them the rank of Major-General, irrespective of their knowledge of English; some of them were *poseurs*, not always detected in the pose, and Steuben was a veritable Münchhausen for mendacity; many of them were preoccupied with their own seniority *vis-à-vis* other Europeans, as Conway was with regard to de Kalb; all of them were indifferent to the effect of their own promotions on the "native" officers.

When Conway became a Major-General of Ordnance, twenty-three native Brigadiers were passed over, including an able "native" in Henry Knox; they all signed a round-robin of protest, and some of them threatened resignation. Washington had too vivid a memory of his own concern over seniority twenty years before, and too much loyalty to his colleagues of this war, to endorse these rapid promotions. They were insisted on by Congress, and they had often to be made by the invention of staff appointments and inspectorships which were no real help to him as Commander. What he wanted, and what he never got, was a plentiful supply of trustworthy field officers. In the grim days at Valley Forge he had to take one of his few good line officers, Greene, and make him Quarter-master to keep the army in being. And yet, after 1777, with the French alliance imminent, all the French "volunteers" (though one at least, de Kalb, began as a French spy) had to be treated with especial solicitude. It was Lafayette's innocence, his willingness to serve without pay, his keenness to lead troops in the field—and perhaps, too, his ability to flatter in a foreign accent—that made him exceptional, and in the end made the relationship of Washington and Lafayette almost that of father and son. But Lafayette's affection was small recompense for the complications and frustrations, and his role has perhaps given an exaggerated importance to the French "volunteers".

If the Conway affair had the good effect of destroying the myth of the sanctity of the "foreigner", it began another myth—the sanctity of Washington. It is true that he was no more obviously successful in the next three years than he had been in the last. But Washington emerged from Valley Forge with a new authority. Behind the patience there was a new fire in the stone, and at Monmouth Court-house it was to erupt and crackle again. Gates' influence was weakened by the difficulties his "Convention" caused, and by his subsequent failures; he went back to the Northern Command on the Hudson in 1778, and was to be, perhaps unjustly, accused of cowardice at Camden in South Carolina in 1780.

Congress had, in the test, supported Washington, and it joined him in deploring the "fatal tendency of disunion". The jealousies and frequent changes in Congress itself weakened what little popular appeal it had. Its currency was unreliable, its executive weak, its officials inexperienced. As the number of Washington's "family" increased with "riding" and "writing" aides, their devotion to him and the Army grew. When France entered the war, and d'Estaing reached the Delaware with twelve ships of the line and several regiments of infantry, Washington was casting off the old hesitations, ready to play a part on the world stage. He was more than ever the leader, less than ever the "Revolutionary", yet increasingly the symbol of the Revolution. He sat to Charles Willson Peale for his portrait. The first reference to Washington as "Des Landes Vater" appears in a German almanac in Pennsylvania in 1779. The seeds of the Washington legend were sown on the bleak hillsides of Valley Forge.

After 1778 the war seemed about to be transformed in one major but simple strategic aspect; it was now to be a war at sea as well as on land. From the beginning, Washington had realised the importance of sea-power, and even put some of his own ill-spared forces on privateers. In 1775 Congress had put what Navy there was under the command of the Yankee Esek Hopkins, who looked much like "an angel, only he swore now and then". The Scots-born John Paul Jones, an ex-slaver turned patriotic pirate, with a squadron of hulks based on Brest and supplied by France, terrorised Britain's coasts, and stole the Earl of Selkirk's silverware in a raid in 1778 on his own "home" waters on the Solway. His activities, greatly embroidered by his own and by others' telling, were not untypical, but, though there were at one time or another two thousand American privateers at sea, they did not seriously threaten the British convoys. They were, in fact, as much a Yankee piece of business as a patriotic venture, and did more to found some early American family fortunes than to supply Washington's army. When France came in, Congress allowed the Navy proper to decline—from thirty-four ships in 1777 to seven in 1781.

The French and Spanish brought 121 ships of the line into the war. Gibraltar was besieged by Spain, Jamaica and the sugar islands were threatened, and in 1780 Mobile and Pensacola seized. A French squadron was active in the Indian Ocean. An invasion of Britain or of Ireland was made possible. John Paul Jones fought an epic fight off Flamborough Head in 1779. The war in America, itself a large-scale raiding, thus far, of Loyalist centres by British armies supplied from the sea, had become a riskier operation. Yet three years were to pass before the French fleet proved of decisive help to the Americans and before French troops were in action. Had d'Estaing not loitered on his journey across the Atlantic, he might have intercepted Clinton's withdrawal from Philadelphia. As it was, his crossing took eighty-eight days, and by the time he reached the Delaware capes, the British fleet was at New York (July 1778). A more resolute man than d'Estaing might even then have attacked the British fleet at Sandy Hook, and in collaboration with Washington, back in White Plains, have made of New York a Yorktown. He refused the attempt and sailed on to Newport, Rhode Island, where an amphibious attack, in combined operations planned with Sullivan, was prevented by bad weather. D'Estaing put back for refitting to Boston. Publicly and politely, Washington wrote to d'Estaing, that "the whole continent sympathises with you". Privately, he thought he had lost a hundred to one chance of ending the war.

The French fleet wintered in the West Indies, picking up, as it were accidentally, some British islands. It failed to return in sufficient force to co-operate with Washington for almost three years. It appeared hurriedly and unexpectedly off Savannah in 1779, and feeble combined operations were attempted against the British; they were costly and unsuccessful. It seems a safe conclusion that there was intent in the hesitations; the French had no wish to win America's independence if it were to leave Britain free to devote herself exclusively to war with France; their motives were Anglophobe rather than libertarian. But the French fleet was, even *in absentia*, a powerful weapon. In 1779, Clinton withdrew his exposed garrison from Rhode Island. Apart from diverting men and ships to the West Indies, this prowling naval force was driving the British armies on land into a policy of contraction. And Washington was ready to seize upon this, ready now not only to hover, as he had put it, but when the moment came to pounce.

The first pounce was indecisive and confused. Clinton retreated from Philadelphia on 18th June 1778, followed by the tattered Continentals. Washington held two Councils of War to consider the wisdom of attacking him; Charles Lee, now exchanged, advised against it; Washington himself favoured a partial blow at the British rear-guard. The attack took place at Monmouth Court-house (28th June 1778). After some hesitation, Lee took command, found the redcoats well posted and, after desultory firing, withdrew; when Washington arrived with the main body, he had to stem a retreat as well as to beat off Clinton. The honours rested with the British; though there were 300 casualties on each side, Clinton withdrew his forces to New York without further difficulty. Washington's men had, however, shown that they could hold their own with bayonet and musket against the Guards themselves.

For Lee, Monmouth brought humiliation. Washington lost his temper with him when he found his forces retreating. According to Lafayette he called Lee "a damned poltroon" —but Lafayette was recollecting this forty-seven years later; it seems likely that the language was something stronger. General Scott, who had a reputation of his own for profanity, was lyrical in his description : "Yes, sir, he swore on that day till the leaves shook on the trees, charming, delightfully. Never have I enjoyed such swearing before or since. Sir, on that memorable day he swore like an angel from Heaven." Unfortunately, Scott was not present when Washington met Lee. As usual, the facts seem to have been either softened or lyricised. Washington in his official communiqués deplored swearing—but was now and then caught in it. It was a hot day and tempers were strained.

The whole thing would probably have been forgotten had not Lee written a biting letter of complaint. He was then formally accused of disobedience of orders, of shameful retreat before the enemy and of disrespect for the Commander-in-Chief. He was court-martialled, found guilty and removed from the Army. He took no further part in the war, and died obscurely in Philadelphia in 1782. Many years later it was discovered that during his period of captivity by the British he had offered Howe plans for ending the war quickly. The charitable explanation of what at one moment appears as egomania and at another as treason or cowardice is that of Elias Boudinot, who knew him well, that he was from the first mentally unbalanced, a paranoiac.

Monmouth proved to be the last major battle in the North. The Continental Army wintered at Middlebrook (1778–9) and again (1779–80) at Morristown, the latter a misery quite as acute as Valley Forge. With the French in the war, the Continental dollar lower than ever in buying power, and profits in privateering, in business and on the farms ever higher, it was increasingly difficult for Washington to keep an army together. It was not by this time a matter of poor organisation, but "the total emptiness of our magazines everywhere, and the total want of money or credit to replenish them". Looting and desertion were common, and they were checked by the sternest of measures, as Corporal Ebenezer Wild tells in his *Journal* :

"The two criminals were brought from the Provest under a strong guard. Their coffins were borne just before them. The Dead March was played behind them . . . Where the Brigade was paraded, the Criminals were brought in front for everyone to see them, after which their sentences was [*sic*] read, which was to be shot. The coffins were set down by the edge of their graves. The men who were to be their executioners had their guns loaded for that purpose, and marched up to within a rod of the coffins. The criminals were made to kneel . . . but at the moment they were to be shot their reprieves were read. The brigade marched back to our camp and was dismissed."

Schuyler and Sullivan, Hamilton and Aaron Burr, ceased to serve. Even the Virginians Morgan and Monroe resigned their commissions. Mutinies broke out among Pennsylvanian and New Jersey troops over lack of pay (January 1781), to be put down only by lavish promises and the threat of attack by more faithful regiments.

Curbing his instincts, Washington held to his defensive

strategy; so, with less wisdom, did Clinton, even though Germain in 1779 urged him to launch just one major attack on Washington. By not doing so, Clinton played Washington's game, for time and the French were on his side. By 1779 Clinton's "policy" was coming to be one of conspiracy, of intermittent raids and of a major campaign in the South.

The line between patriot and Loyalist had been blurred in 1776, and to many in the Middle States it was still blurred in 1779. Though many estimates, beginning with John Adams', have put the numbers of the Loyalists at one-third and of the passive at another third of the population, these figures seem in fact conservative for the area between the Hudson and the Potomac, the Tory Heartland. The historian Van Tyne puts the number of Loyalists who fought for Britain as high as 50,000. There were in all sixty-nine Loyalist regiments, though only twenty-one of them had numbers to warrant this title. One thousand Loyalists had left New York for Halifax with Howe in 1776, three thousand more left Philadelphia with the British in 1778—the refugees of the American Revolution. Most of those who stayed behind, and were rash enough to declare their sympathies, suffered in property and person—there are many stories of tar and feathers. Double spies abounded, especially in New York. In this environment, it was natural that the British should seek to persuade Americans secretly as well as openly to change their allegiance—or, from another point of view, to persuade them to stay true to their older allegiance. The Howes had used the pardoning power skilfully and openly in the Jerseys in 1776. Clinton used it again in 1779.

What was permissible, however, for civilians, often poor, bewildered and afraid, was another matter for soldiers. Treason and desertion in Washington's army were punishable by death. Rumours of treason had circulated already, with reference to Charles Lee and Joseph Reed. Hickey, of Washington's guard at Cambridge in 1776, had already paid the price. In 1780 treason reached its climax.

On 23rd September three American volunteer militiamen near Tarrytown, New York, surprised a young man in civilian clothes trying to get through their lines towards New York. They searched him, probably for loot, and found papers that revealed an alarming plot. The man was John André, Clinton's Adjutant-General, who was returning from a meeting with Benedict Arnold, the most dashing and one of the ablest of American commanders. The papers revealed that Arnold was ready to surrender West Point on the Hudson, the centre of the American defensive arc running from Morristown to White Plains, for £10,000. André was tried at Washington's headquarters, and hanged as a spy; Arnold escaped to become a British General—and in America a synonym for traitor. His memorial at Saratoga, a boot on an unmarked monument, suggests that only the leg in which he was twice wounded is worthy of respect. Among the tablets in the Old Cadet Chapel at West Point, listing the names of all the Revolutionary Generals, is a nameless marble inscribed "Major-General —— Born 1740 ——".[1]

As a result of this act of treason and of its subsequent dramatisation by Americans, Arnold's services—and his tragedy—have perhaps been lost to sight. His march up the Kennebec, on the plan conceived by Washington, his gallantry at Quebec, where he was wounded, at Ridgefield and at Saratoga, where he was wounded again, none of these had brought him the credit to which he rightly felt entitled. He was greatly admired by Washington, but he had influential enemies in Congress; in 1777, despite Washington's protests, five of his inferiors in rank were promoted over his head.

His defection has sometimes been explained by his bitterly anti-French sentiments and his dislike for the alliance with France; sometimes more romantically by the fact that in the spring of 1779, while serving as military commander in Philadelphia, he had married a Tory belle, the eighteen-year-old Peggy Shippen, daughter of a Philadelphia loyalist, and had run up huge debts for her sake; André has at times even been cast in the role of rival lover. There is no real evidence for these views. The correspondence with Clinton had been going on for sixteen months, and Arnold's wife appears to have been fully involved in it from the beginning.

It began after he became embroiled with the civil authorities in Philadelphia, where he was defrauding the Army by

[1] For a fascinating account of the treachery of Arnold, and others, see Carl Van Doren: *Secret History of the American Revolution* (Viking Press, New York, 1941).

trading in clothing supplies, living luxuriously and spending wildly—he bought the Mount Pleasant estate on the Schuyl-kill for his bride. Every effort was made to hush the scandal, for officers of his combative temperament were rare. But the sympathy came too late and was perhaps misunderstood. Arnold was thirty-nine, ambitious, quarrelsome, embittered; like many another in the American and the British ranks, he was a professional trader who had turned his talents to the game of war and found it rich in opportunities for private profit at public expense; though braver and abler than most of his colleagues (on both sides), he believed only in himself and in putting a financial estimate on his talents. Franklin expressed what has become the verdict of history on Arnold, when he said that Judas received thirty pieces of silver for selling one man, but Arnold, who tried to sell three million, received less than one cent per head.

"Few men have virtue to withstand the highest bidder," Washington had said the year before. But it was, after all, a civil war, in which loyalties were confused, and few of the major participants were unmercenary. Treason did not stop with Arnold, or with Aaron Burr in 1805. Similar but totally unsuccessful invitations to treachery were made to Ethan Allen, Philip Schuyler, Israel Putnam and John Sullivan. None was made or was likely to be made to Washington.

Conspiracy having failed, Clinton then began a policy of plundering raids, in which local Tories participated, on New England towns like New Bedford, New Haven and New London (led by Arnold) and in Virginia in 1779–80–81. Though contemporary accounts of these raids were no doubt exaggerated, Clinton himself estimated the damage done in Virginia at £2,000,000. Parts of Connecticut and Westchester County were pillaged, Norwalk and Fairfield burned. As the *New York Packet* commented on a raid on Hackensack— "They distress a few, they can subdue the spirits of none. . . . The spirits of freemen are not to be depressed by horse-thieves, house-breakers and ragamuffins. . . ."

Washington could not prevent these raids, any more than in 1775–6, but to some degree he could repay in kind—"Mad Anthony" Wayne stormed the British fort at Stony Point on the Hudson (July 1779), in a tactically brilliant but otherwise insignificant operation, and "Light-horse" Harry Lee, Washington's cavalry leader and close friend, attacked Paulus Hook in New Jersey (August 1779). More important, Washington sent columns westward, to defend the frontiers of the Northern states against Britain's Indian allies, for, despite Schuyler's efforts to keep the Indians neutral, some of the worst savagery of the war had occurred in 1778 in the Wyoming and Cherry Valley massacres at the hands of the Six Nations, equipped from the British post at Niagara. In 1779 Sullivan defeated the Iroquois at Newtown, systematically and barbarously destroyed their villages, and checked, without finally ending, the Indian threat in New York.

More alarming were the raids carried out by Indian scalping parties from Detroit into the Ohio and Illinois country, which since 1774 had been part of the Province of Quebec. To curb these the Virginian, George Rogers Clark, occupied the old French towns on the Upper Mississippi Valley, captured the British garrison at Vincennes, and, more important, its commander, Henry Hamilton (the "Hair-buyer").

This campaign, sometimes represented as winning "the West" for the United States, was a purely Virginian enterprise, reminiscent, in its heroic marches through "the drowned lands", of Arnold's expedition through the Maine forests. It won Clark a similar ingratitude; neither he nor his men got a cent of pay, and James Wilkinson blackened his reputation for his own purposes. Clark did not get sufficient support from Virginia to attack Detroit, and he did not end Indian threats, least of all north of the Ohio—memories of British-incited Indian raids were still alive in 1812. But to West Virginia, Kentucky and Tennessee, Clark's expedition brought a respite from attack, and it tied them loosely to the fortunes of Virginia, though boundaries, like loyalties, remained uncertain until 1815.

Similarly, between 1778 and 1781, Washington and Congress considered a further drive on Canada, casting Lafayette for the role of leader. The plans in the end came to nothing. The core of the resistance remained in Washington's little army; conspiracy and intrigue, raid and counter-raid, could not hide the essential fact that as long as the Army stayed undefeated and unbroken, resistance continued. When the opportunity came, there was a force poised to take advantage of it, however ill-equipped, unpaid and mutinous it might be.

The opportunity came at last when the British carried the war into what seemed the last stronghold of Loyalism—the South.

In the first years of the war the South had escaped lightly. A British fleet under Clinton and Sir Peter Parker had attempted an attack on Charleston in 1776, to be beaten off by the gunners on Sullivan's Island (Fort Moultrie). Lee by his presence won a renown that properly belonged to Moultrie's palmetto logs and their shell-absorbing softness, and to his gunners—one ball carried away the seat of Sir Peter Parker's pants, and, according to an old ballad, "propeled him along on his bumpus". In 1778, a British force landed in Georgia, captured Savannah and Atlanta, and controlled the state for the rest of the war. In 1780 a force of 14,000 men sailed from New York under Clinton and Cornwallis, slipped past Sullivan's Island in a storm, and successfully besieged the city—5,000 Americans under General Lincoln surrendered.

From Charleston, Cornwallis began the most serious and sustained effort of the war to defeat the patriot forces, to set up Loyalist civil governments and to regain at least part of America for Britain. This was the old plan of "divide and conquer", with a view now to the detaching of the South, the "promised land of Tories". Luzerne, the French Minister in America, drew the conclusion that Britain was preparing to abandon the Northern states and to form a new government of the two Carolinas, Georgia, East Florida and the Bahamas : "a respectable possession", he thought.

Had the methods tried in loyalist Georgia been applied to the South as a whole, they might have been successful. In practice, the war in the South became, the Indian horrors and P.O.W. ships excepted, the most frightful chapter in a struggle conducted thus far with a certain eighteenth-century humanity. Banastre Tarleton's cavalry raiders were often vicious, as at Waxhaws and Rocky Mount, and made implacable enemies, among them young Andrew Jackson; the patriot forces replied in kind at Hanging Rock and King's Mountain. The Hessians, little used for two years, were active in the siege of Charleston, and still had the reputation of pillagers. Civilians were plundered, in their homes, in their negro slaves and in their own persons; rebel leaders like

Gadsden were dragged away to prison ships; in the west a self-generated militia movement arose, the "over-mountain men" with leaders like John Sevier and Isaac Shelby, who have left their memorials in the historical markers along the Wateree and Broad Rivers of South Carolina; menacing the redcoats in the lowlands were Thomas Sumter, Andrew Pickens and Francis Marion, "the swamp fox". This Southern militia, buttressed by Continental troops from Washington's army, fought in fact a guerrilla war. "There was scarce an inhabitant between the Santee and the Pee Dee that was not in arms against us," said Cornwallis.

Thus the British victories in the South are less impressive than they appear. Nevertheless, in 1780 Cornwallis ran into and destroyed a superior American force under Gates at Camden. Gates retreated precipitately, leaving North Carolina exposed, and was replaced by Nathanael Greene. Never happy as a Quarter-master, Greene was ready to fight the war in the South on the Washington model, and indeed, unlike Gates, was "subject to the control of the Commander-in-Chief". The Army was now co-ordinated. The object was not to win battles but to avoid defeats, to draw Cornwallis away from Charleston and his naval supply route, to use "Light-horse Harry" Lee's cavalry to counter Tarleton's, and to attack isolated units with guerrillas.

Tarleton was defeated at Cowpens (January 1781). Cornwallis reached the Dan, on the boundaries of south-western Virginia, and fought a pitched battle at Guilford Courthouse, a British victory of the sort that ruins an army—"A pledge," said Tarleton, "of ultimate defeat." It was a war of chase and manœuvre, a "Country Dance" with the British led at last by a commander who sought decisions. He took his army to Wilmington, and in April 1781, to Clinton's consternation, marched into Virginia.

In the previous two years there had been four raids into Virginia up the tidal rivers, one of them led by Arnold; Richmond, and Petersburg with its stores of tobacco, and some plantation homes, had been burnt. Virginia's waterways made it vulnerable to invasion, but little had been done to prepare its defences; its Governor, Jefferson, was happier as a theorist than as an executive. And it offered tempting booty. Cornwallis drove into Richmond, and Tarleton's cavalry almost captured the Governor at Charlottesville—he rode down one side of his little mountain as Tarleton galloped up the other. Lafayette took up the game of dodging and parrying. Cornwallis moved towards the sea to be near the British fleet, and in July set up defences on the Yorktown peninsula.

The idea of bottling up the British in Virginia had presented itself already, and Washington had lost his temper when it failed against Arnold through what he thought the lethargy of the French. In 1781 he had some 5,000 Continentals in New York, and he was joined by Rochambeau with some 5,000 French, brought from Newport. In July they pressed the new French naval commander in the West Indies, the Comte de Grasse, to sail for the Chesapeake and to attempt a combined operation. When he agreed, Washington and Rochambeau began to move their forces southward to trap Cornwallis (17th August). Though they tried to hide their intentions from Clinton, he informed Cornwallis (2nd September) that Virginia was the probable target. The Virginian Major St. George Tucker exulted—"We shall have a Burgoyneade in Virginia. . . ."

Washington did not find it so easy to exult. He marched his men through Philadelphia, and their numbers raised a dust "like a smothering snow-storm"; but alongside the French regiments they were unkempt and ill-disciplined, and they had not been paid for months. It was only the news of de Grasse's arrival off the Chesapeake that enabled Robert Morris to pay them, and this he did by borrowing a month's pay from Rochambeau himself. To confirm that the Fates were smiling on American efforts, the *Résolue* reached Boston with two million livres from France—and the casks of coins were dragged over New England and New Jersey roads to Philadelphia. Washington was in his own country now, seeing familiar orchards and fields golden with the finest crops for seven years. He paused at Mount Vernon before taking command at Williamsburg on 15th September.

Even then his difficulties were not over, and de Grasse gave him more trouble than Cornwallis. With forty ships of the line, de Grasse defeated a relieving force under Admiral Graves on 5th September, and wanted to continue the struggle at sea. He had no taste for a passive role in a war of sieges—and wanted to return to the West Indies. A conference was held on his flagship, *Ville de Paris*, which seven months later was to be a riddled hulk at the Battle of the Saints; he finally gave way to Washington's pleas, but he still refused to station frigates above Cornwallis' position, and left him therefore a thin and desperate chance of escape. It was not taken, however; on land, outnumbered at least two to one, and outgunned, cut off from his sea supplies, and with the parallels and approaches pushing steadily nearer, Cornwallis capitulated on 17th October, seven days before relief ships appeared and four years to the day after Burgoyne's surrender.

Washington refused to consider a convention like that at Saratoga, and gave identical terms to those offered by Clinton to Lincoln at Charleston in 1780, total surrender. Lincoln was appointed to receive Cornwallis' sword, but the latter pleaded illness, and the surrender on the 19th was formally made by General O'Hara.

For the second time in the war an entire British Army was lost at one stroke, and with it 7,241 men, 214 cannon, 6,658 muskets, 457 horses, 30 transports and over £2,000 in cash. When the British marched out to stack their arms, they seemed to more than one observer arrogant and "much in liquor". And a band played "The world turned upside-down". It was the end of the fighting in America.

Not that this was in any way apparent at the time to Washington, harassed by the recurrent problems of scarcity and disease, and grieving over Jacky Custis, dead at Yorktown. He tried, unsuccessfully, to persuade de Grasse to attempt similar operations against Charleston. He sent his main force back to the Hudson, believing that the greatest military effort would be needed in 1782—there were still 16,000 British troops in New York and 9,000 in the Carolinas. While the issue was being decided in Virginia, Greene was driving the British from the Carolinas into Charleston, in a series of engagements that mark him out as one of the few able strategists of the war. The British finally withdrew from Charleston in December 1782.

After Yorktown, *en route* North, Washington spent fifteen weeks in Philadelphia; weeks of formal dinners in the French style, of hunting, of music and a play in his honour. It was for him the least warlike period of the struggle.

Despite his warnings against any relaxation of effort, America became a bystander in the war, as news poured in of further British disasters—the loss of St. Eustatius, the Dutch supply-point in the Caribbean which Rodney had captured in 1781; the loss of Nevis and St. Kitts and Montserrat in the West Indies; and then Minorca. With each loss the ministerial majority in the House of Commons fell, and as Stedman, the contemporary British historian, put it, the war was now "generally disrelished". With only three islands in the West Indies remaining to Britain, Lord North resigned (March 1782). For a moment, George III considered abdication.

Rockingham took office on an understanding that peace must be made with America, even at the cost of independence. Richard Oswald was sent to Paris to open negotiations with Franklin. Carleton replaced Clinton as Commander in New York, and showed himself again generous and conciliatory; Washington remained sceptical of his approaches. Every ship brought different reports—of Rodney's victory over de Grasse in the West Indies in April, of Rockingham's death in July. Not until December 1782 was it clear that Britain had tacitly admitted that the struggle was over; she had authorised peace commissioners to treat with the "Thirteen United States of America". In March 1783 came the news that the provisional treaty had been signed in Paris in November.

The treaty was made without official consultation with France, though with that country's complete knowledge, thanks to the efficiency of her spies. American independence was recognised, and the Mississippi (not the Appalachians, as the Spanish had hoped) was fixed as the Western boundary. Congress was to urge the states to restore to the loyalists the properties they had lost, an obligation only Franklin's Pennsylvania sought to honour. For the United States it was total success. It included the broad territories formerly part of Quebec Province, the southern fringes of which had been won by George Rogers Clark—now the states of Michigan, Illinois, Ohio, Indiana and Wisconsin. Well could Washington salute on the eighth anniversary of Lexington "this stupendous fabric of freedom and empire on the broad basis of independency". Spain in the end kept the Floridas and Minorca, and for the next twelve years controlled the mouth of the Mississippi. Britain retained Gibraltar and doubled her national debt. France acquired a few West Indian islands, the prestige of defeating her ancient enemy and of dividing the English-speaking world; she achieved also a condition of near-bankruptcy that brought a more violent revolution in its train. Certainly the world of 1775 had been transformed.

For Washington and his army, however, as for most commanders, the pattern was slow to clarify, the satisfactions easier to appreciate in retrospect. The men quartered at West Point and at Newburgh would not go home until they were paid, and there was nothing with which to pay them. Nor did the government set up by the Articles of Confederation, and finally approved by the states in 1781, have sufficient strength for tired men to trust paper promises to pay in the remote future.

It was in this mood that the dangers foreseen in 1778 by John Adams and Benjamin Rush recurred. In May 1782 Colonel Lewis Nicola, a supply officer, invited Washington to play a greater role—"I believe strong arguments might be produced for admitting the title of King." Washington viewed the proposal "with abhorrence" and reprehended it "with severity. . . ." "If I am not deceived in the knowledge of myself, you could not have found a person to whom your schemes are more disagreeable." The last threat to American republicanism was ended not at Yorktown but at Newburgh.

Washington was equally firm in appealing to the patriotism of the officers to resist the temptation implied in the anonymous Newburgh Addresses of March 1783, urging the army to take justice into its own hands. In General Orders, he denounced this "irregular invitation" and addressed the officers in person—for him no easy task. He found his manuscript hard to decipher, and had to put on his spectacles —"Gentlemen, you must pardon me. I have grown gray in your service and now find myself growing blind." The observation was effective—so much so that later cynics have suggested it was done deliberately for its emotional effect; it seems unlikely in a commander so little given to histrionics.

The officers thanked him and expressed a confidence in the justice of Congress that was rooted in fact in trust in their leader. It was the first and only time that the Commander and the Army clashed.

After an appeal by Washington, Congress voted the Continental officers full compensation for five years, instead of half-pay for life, as promised earlier. Efforts were made to scrape together three months' pay for the men, but most of them went off to their homes, as Washington reported, without a farthing in their pockets.

There was no parade, no last review. The Continental Army disappeared as it came, on foot, in little groups, along country roads, begging for food. Washington took a more sentimental farewell of his officers at Fraunces' Tavern in New York, where the memory of the long ordeal brought tears and embraces. He moved south, in triumphal style, church bells ringing and thirteen-gun salutes greeting him. In December 1783, at Annapolis, with a hand that shook visibly, he resigned "with satisfaction" an appointment he had accepted "with diffidence". Congress expressed its thanks. He had, however, no doubts who the real heroes were. As he wrote to Greene, the future historian would find it hard to believe "that such a force as Great Britain has employed for eight years in this country could be baffled in their plan of subjugating it, by numbers infinitely less, composed of men oftentimes half starved, always in rags, without pay, and experiencing every species of distress, which human nature is capable of undergoing".

The mystery continues to baffle the historian. Britain had infinitely greater resources than America. She outweighed her four-to-one in manpower, a hundred-to-one in fighting ships. Even after the entry of France, Washington wrote to Joseph Reed urging caution and realism—"the maritime resources of Britain", he argued, "are more substantial and real than those of France and Spain united . . . in modern wars the longest purse must chiefly determine the event". Until 1778 at least, control of the seas gave British forces the equivalent of interior lines with the ability to concentrate at points of their own choosing. When Canada was invaded in 1775–6 it was easier to reinforce British troops in Quebec from London than to reinforce the Americans overland from New York. Even after 1778 Britain still controlled the seas, though erratically and with one fatal lapse in 1781. A war of blockade could hardly have failed, but it was never attempted.

France fought the war as a sea-power, in which she was inferior in skill and training to Britain; and she put only 9,000 troops into America, a few regiments in 1778, 5,000 men under Rochambeau (1780) and 3,000 from the West Indies in de Grasse's ships for Yorktown (1781). She greatly assisted the American cause with subsidies and supplies (some eight million dollars in all), but she did this before 1778 as well as after. What she was seeking was revenge on Britain and the conquest of West Indian islands rather than American independence, and in practice she gave that cause little assistance. The war could still have been won by the United Colonies without any formal entry of France or Spain.

The explanation of the American war is not that Washington won it but that Britain lost it, and to the terrain rather than to the enemy. She began it in 1775 with divided counsels, and by 1778 many more groups, especially the merchants, had ceased to echo the King's sentiments. Her commanders reflected the hesitations at home, sometimes for liberal reasons. Amherst refused an American command, Keppel accepted the call as Admiral only when France became the enemy. The Howe brothers, skilful though they were in their elements, were second cousins of George III, and were charged to play the role of conciliators as well as commanders; they never struck home—as they could have done in New York and the Jerseys in 1776. One cynical English view of Howe was that he should be raised to the peerage as Baron "Delay Warr". Clinton's recently published *Narrative* of his campaigns reveals a shy and dilatory man, his moods alternating between timidity and aggressive confidence. Burgoyne was an ineffective commander, who paid the price at Saratoga of culpable over-confidence. Cornwallis marred a decisiveness that brought false hopes in London by recklessness in invading Virginia, and farther south by condoning pillage and plunder that fostered a guerrilla war; the campaign in the Carolinas was fought in country ill-suited to war, and was won by the patriots in a score of small engagements marked by heavy losses. Carleton came to full command too late; his nobility impressed many Americans; his skill kept Canada loyal. Only Carleton condemned the plundering raids of Indians, of Tories and of British regulars, which were in the end a matter of approved and unfortunate British strategy.

The obligation to win the war rested on the British commanders on the spot, and they failed to honour it, failed indeed for five years to show any inclination to do so. Germain in London gave full discretion and full support to them. The war was caused by political failures in London, and it was lost by military failures in America.

There were some sound tactical movements, mainly of Howe's, and British artillery and cavalry were superior to American. The country, however, was utterly different from the Europe in which the art of war had been practised— forested, humid, intersected by malarial creeks and swamps, short of roads and bridges. There were, as a result, some remarkable military disasters; in the war as a whole there were fourteen actions in which the defeated force was either captured entire or destroyed, and in nine of these the better-supplied, better-disciplined British Army was the victim— Moore's Creek, Trenton, Bennington, Saratoga, Vincennes, Stony Point, King's Mountain, Cowpens, Yorktown. Three of these, Trenton, Saratoga and Yorktown, were psychological or military turning-points, and two of them were won by Washington. In these nine engagements, the British losses, exceeding 20,000, were sufficiently serious to be decisive in a war waged on a small scale.

The employment of Hessians was unwise. They caused trouble in the Jerseys, they themselves resented the pride and arrogance of the English regular officers, and they showed little adaptation to American conditions. General Haldimand, writing to Clinton from Quebec in 1779, thought "the Germans were unfit by nature and education for the American service". By contrast, the British were slow to use the Loyalists, despite their optimism about them, and few Loyalist leaders of military capacity emerged.

Though superior to the Americans in tactics and in the set battles of the war, the British troops failed to adjust themselves to the terrain, and were unable to maintain themselves for long at any distance from the sea.

Unlike the British, Washington's Army was civilian and unprofessional, the first people's army. Recruited haphazardly, rarely numbering more than 10,000 after 1775, as many as two-thirds might be local militia and undependable —"the Long Faces". They "come in," said Washington, "you cannot tell how; go, you cannot tell when; and act, you cannot tell where; consume your provisions, exhaust your stores and leave you at last at the critical moment". Yet he had constantly to magnify his numbers and to minimise his losses if he was to maintain the country's morale. This led to Congressional alarm lest the military seize the initiative. Washington had to use his dictatorial powers carefully and to placate Congress over eight difficult years.

His Army was short of everything—Franklin proposed in the beginning that the Pennsylvania troops be equipped with bows and arrows, Indian style. Problems of supply and clothing were not overcome until 1782, even with French aid; even then there was never enough clothing for the men to be "deloused"; pay was short, winters appalling. It took three years before the appropriate drill was devised and before officers as well as men were persuaded by Steuben to learn it; it took longer for cavalry and artillery to be used skilfully. Washington deplored the desertions and the cowardice of his men, especially at the beginning; but much more than this he deplored the lack of able officers—"Our men," agreed Greene, "are infinitely better than the officers." But the officers emerged : "Light-horse Harry" and his cavalry, Morgan and his riflemen, John Glover and his marines, Greene and Knox, Wayne and Stirling.

The Continental Army was created by Washington. Though Congress gave him more assistance than has usually been recognised, nevertheless it remains true that Washington was the Army, and at times only the existence of an Army kept the Revolution alive—"the Atlas of America, and the god of the army : his authority is gentle and paternal," wrote the Chevalier de Fleury in 1779. It was Washington who persuaded Congress to create the Continental Line, who badgered Congress for reinforcements and supplies and pay, and when these failed held it together by force and his own money (in 1776), by example and drill (at Valley Forge) and by discipline (increasingly and persistently). He had no illusions—he was, he said in 1780, "living upon expedients".

It is true that he never defeated the main British Army in the open; he was more successful as an administrator than as a trainer of men; at times he was hesitant and too deferential to his fellow-generals. He lacked Lee's *flair* and Arnold's dash; but he also lacked their faults. Though tactically he was never more than an amateur, yet he made distinct contributions to the art of war : the use of light infantry and skirmishers; the employment of riflemen; the fondness for manœuvre rather than sieges and particularly for manœuvre at night (sometimes forced upon him); the effort at combined operations. For one with so little experience, he was daring and surprisingly resilient, "much bolder in spirit", says Freeman, "than circumstances permitted him to be in strategy". This strategy was inevitably defensive, and there was no glory to be won—or volunteers to be enlisted—in a policy of retreat, a war of posts; no glory, much criticism and a recurring, humiliating sense of failure. Yet to survive was in the end to conquer : as Greene expressed it in the South in 1781 : "Don't you think that we bear beating very well, and that . . . the more we are beat, the better we grow?"

Washington got little permanent help from other generals; the American War, like many others, was ruthless with reputations. Of the original "natives" only the stiff-legged Greene and the stentor-voiced Knox grew in stature as it proceeded and in the trust that Washington reposed in them. There is some evidence, not yet fully explored, that even Greene was touched by peculation. Out of the association with the fat Boston bookseller, Henry Knox, whose weight nearly upset the barge crossing the Delaware, grew one of Washington's firmest friendships and the Society of the Cincinnati. Of the "foreigners", only Lafayette won Washington's close friendship, and his reputation has probably been inflated by that fact and by his subsequent career. Rochambeau at the siege of Yorktown and by his skill in handling de Grasse rendered greater service to the cause than Lafayette, and was self-effacing, as Lafayette was not.

Among all of these, native and foreign, the sensitive and the super-sensitive, the troublesome and the ambitious, the generous and the grasping, only Washington moves as completely just and completely trustworthy, infinitely patient, inflexibly determined, giving way now and then to petulance and temper, and to wild anger when he met treachery, expressing now and then, like Lincoln, his liking for men who would fight, or, like Robert E. Lee, his liking for Virginians; but throughout, amid all the details, seeing the war as a whole and embodying its purposes. After Valley Forge, the natural dignity and the calm bearing of the man had become symbolic of the cause.

Chapter Seven

Cincinnatus: The Critical Period
(1783 — 1789)

" A T length, My dear Marquis," Washington wrote to
Lafayette, "I am become a private citizen on the banks
of the Potomac, and under the shadow of my own vine and
my own fig-tree." Except for brief visits *en route* to and
from Yorktown, he had been absent from Mount Vernon for
eight and a half years—years which had aged and tired him,
despite his muscular strength and his tall frame.

There was little immediate relaxation. The resumption of
prodigal entertaining; the obligations incumbent on a Virginian squire, now without secretaries, to advise and assist
all who pestered him; the "applications, enquiries and the
letters of compliment, as unmeaning as they are troublesome"; these were heavy burdens. In 1785 he hired a secretary, William Shaw, to write and "methodise" his papers,
and replaced him a year later by the loyal and unselfish
Tobias Lear. And fame brought portrait painters and sculp-
tors to Mount Vernon, including Houdon from Paris.
Eighteen months were to elapse after his return before he
was able to write in his diary that he had dined alone with
Martha.

He was saddened, too, by the deaths of friends, and recur-
rently preoccupied, as his letters show, with the idea of
death. In 1781 the Loyalist Lord Fairfax had died in the
Valley, some said of a broken heart when he heard the news
that his protégé Washington had captured an army of his
King at Yorktown; and in 1786 the Virginian Assembly
abolished the great proprietary. When "camp fever" carried
off "Jacky" Custis in the same year, Washington adopted
two of his four children, George Washington Parke Custis,
who built Arlington House and whose *Recollections* are

responsible for many of the Washington legends, and Eleanor Custis, who was truly a daughter to him in his last years. General Greene, and his aide, Tench Tilghman, died in 1786. In the spring of 1787 died his favourite brother, John Augustine—"the intimate companion of my youth, and the friend of my ripened age".

The years had left their mark also on Mount Vernon; it had been managed in Washington's absence by his kinsman, Lund Washington, and he had made no money from it. What debts were due were being paid off in depreciated "Continentals" worth at most a sixpence in the pound. Washington had served in the war without pay and had little to invest. He had been meticulous in keeping a ledger of his expenses—they included an account of Martha's expenses, too, in visiting him at headquarters each winter—over eight years, and they were met by Congress in full and without question; but this was small recompense.

It was not long, however, before the old interests were resumed—of landowner, prudent and scientific manager and venturous speculator. His years in the North confirmed his belief that a single-crop tobacco plantation was too risky, especially without a guaranteed market in Britain. He continued to diversify the crops with barley and wheat, oranges and peas. He experimented with seed, and he fought against the erosion of Mount Vernon's thin soils. By 1786 there were six plantations, each with an overseer in charge, and with some three hundred slaves in all. These farms were visited each day, a twenty-mile ride.

He took up again his interest in a trade route West along the Potomac, and the idea of a canal link with the Ohio; and in 1785 the Potomac Navigation Company was born after a conference held at Mount Vernon between Virginia and Maryland representatives.

In 1784, with his nephew Bushrod and his old friend Dr. Craik, he visited his lands in the West, again to travel over Braddock's Road to Great Meadows and Fort Necessity, and again to meet old Tom Cresap, the Indian trader, grown prosperous on frontier booty. There is little trace in Washington's diary, or his letters, of emotion recollected in tranquillity, no time wasted on reminiscence or nostalgia. He found squatters on his land, and when they refused to buy at his price he determined to assert the rights of landlord. Formerly he had instructed his agents to avoid clashes with those who occupied land to which they were not entitled; with "a society of Cececders" who had gone west during the War, he had no sympathy. The lawsuit that followed dragged on for two years, but Washington won in the end. The settlers were evicted, and he acquired not only the cleared land but the improvements they had made on it; what had cost him originally fifty-five dollars plus the cost of the survey was sold for twelve thousand. He profited similarly from the sale of land on the Mohawk which he had bought in partnership with Governor Clinton of New York in 1782.

If to Mount Vernon and to his success in land speculation are added his houses in Alexandria and Williamsburg and the increase in the number of his slaves by births, Washington was one of the wealthiest Americans, at his death the owner of some sixty thousand acres; yet, like many other planters, he rarely had enough cash to meet his needs. "My estate for the last eleven years," he wrote in 1787, "has not been able to make both ends meet." Even so, he refused to accept any grant of land from Congress for his military services in the war; land speculation was a general and a legitimate activity, a promise to undertake voluntary public service, however wearing, was another matter. The ethics of the man of business did not conflict with the code of the gentleman-farmer.

The western journey was not merely a landowner's inspection. The western problem involved something more than the enhancement of land values along the Potomac; involved more, too, than the inheritance of Britain's old dilemma—conflict between migrants and Indian tribes in the great area between the Alleghenies and the Mississippi. It was a problem in statesmanship. Spain, by treaty and possession, controlled the mouth of the West's natural highway, the Mississippi; Britain had not yet surrendered the posts which guarded the northern boundary with Canada and which protected a fur trade worth £100,000 per year. Sandwiched between Spain and Britain and lacking roads to the East, the unmapped territories across the mountains were the stakes of the next generation's diplomacy; the thirteen independent and not yet united states in the East must manœuvre for control of the West against Great Powers old in intrigue.

On this issue, however, the thirteen states had strong sectional feelings; having lost Canadian, West Indian and British markets, the North-east wanted a revival of trade, on any terms, with Spain or with other countries, and was ready to accept the closing of the Mississippi if it were necessary. John Jay made an agreement with Spain in 1786 along these lines. The West was outraged, feeling it had been literally sold down the river, and intrigues (in which James Wilkinson reappears) as well as tempers, mounted. Though Virginian delegates in Congress supported the West, and though Washington saw the danger that the West might by "demagogues" be driven to "acts of extravagance and desperation", he supported the agreement. It would compel, he thought, the construction of a Potomac–Ohio canal, and drive the West to consider closer union with the East. Congress rejected the treaty by a sectional vote, the seven Northern states supporting it but failing to muster the nine votes needed for adoption.

This issue revealed once more the dangers of American sectionalism and the weaknesses of Congress. New England was not interested in the South-West. The free land in the West would draw Americans like a magnet, but when they settled there they might lose whatever thin traditions of "loyalty" to the East they ever had. It was likely to happen even without Spanish bribery and without American "traitors". The West for its part thought it was being sacrificed to traders and speculators. Here were the roots of the Spanish Conspiracy of 1797, of the Burr Conspiracy of 1805 and in part of the War of 1812.

Washington appreciated this problem long before most of his contemporaries. "There is nothing which binds one country or one state to another but interest," he wrote to Richard Henry Lee. "Without this cement the western inhabitants who more than probably will be composed in a great degree of foreigners, can have no predilection for us, and a commercial connexion is the only tie we can have upon them." This was percipient, but it was not, of course, the whole truth. The Ordinances of 1785 and of 1787—providing for surveys, the organisation of townships and the ultimate erection of territorial and state governments in the West on terms of equality with those already in being in the East—were perhaps more effective than acts or routes of trade in linking the fortunes of the future western states to the eastern seaboard. But Washington was, along with Jefferson, one of the first to see the political challenge and involvement of the western territories, and the dangers of secession in the West. As so many American historians forget, the identification of the western areas with the East was not automatic; it called for deft diplomacy, it was marred by intrigue and treachery, and it was not finally accomplished until 1815.

Washington resumed then his western as well as his planter interests. And the conference at Mount Vernon, between Maryland and Virginia, to discuss the future of the Potomac, was the beginning of a new sequence of events, an opportunity and a portent. Practically all the states had similar boundary problems to resolve : New York, New Hampshire and Massachusetts still fought, as they had done during the war, for control of Vermont, and Pennsylvanians attacked Connecticut settlers in the Wyoming Valley as though they were Indians. When the disputes were not over boundaries or western land, they were over tariffs or currency—New York taxed farm imports from Connecticut and New Jersey. And they stemmed from one central fact— the powerlessness of Congress under the Articles of Confederation (1781).

Patriotic American historians since 1787, seeking to justify the Constitution of that year, have made much of the weakness of the government provided by the Articles. They have accepted the constant pleading of Washington during the war as a political indictment of Congress; the *Federalist* of Madison, Hamilton and Jay, designed as propaganda in favour of the Constitution, has been regarded as a Book of Revelation; since John Fiske used the term in 1888, the period from 1781–9 has become known as "The Critical Period" and its political achievements have been minimised: the waging of the war and the winning of the peace, the abolition of slavery in the North-West, the drafting of the Ordinances for the government of the West—the first appli-

cation of the principles of 1776 to the government of conquered territory, a Declaration, not only of Independence
but of non-imperialism. More recently, in the writing of
Max Farrand, Charles Warren and Merrill Jensen, there has
been an effort to see the Articles in terms of the years 1776–
81, and in terms of the highly democratic theory by which
the Revolution was fought. The commercial crisis was due,
these writers have stressed, not to the Articles but to the dis-
location of trade relations with foreign countries. The fiscal
difficulties in 1785, as in 1765, were due to the unwillingness
of Americans to be taxed by a remote authority, whether at
home or abroad. The years of crisis were also in some
measure years of prosperity.

Nevertheless, the severance of the tie with Britain in 1776
did leave the Americans a disunited people in thirteen distinct
commonwealths. During the war, Washington's Army rather
than Congress was the effective centre of unity. The states
were reluctant to surrender their hardly won powers. Since
so much of revolutionary feeling was localised, it was hard
to transform it into a national cause, a *levée en masse*, as
Washington found. His proclamation in 1776 requiring all
who had taken an oath of allegiance to Britain either to take
an oath of allegiance to the United States of America or to
be treated as common enemies had been thought of by some
Congressmen as a dangerous assumption of power, an infringement on the rights of the states.

Neither the Articles nor the war produced an American
"nation" or a national citizenship; Jefferson was not alone
in believing that "that government is best which governs
least". The Articles of Confederation agreed upon by Congress in 1777 were not ratified until 1781; Maryland refused
to accept them unless the seven states with Western lands
turned over their land claims to the central government.
What they established was a loose confederation, "a league
of friendship", a collection of ambassadors rather than a
government.

Under the Articles, there was no President in the sense of
a distinct executive; Congress exercised legislative, executive
and judicial functions all in one. Each state had one vote;
nine votes were needed to carry any measure, and all thirteen were needed to carry an amendment to the Articles.

Congress could not bind individuals or states; it could only persuade, exhort and encourage—or the reverse. It could not tax—it laid a financial quota on each state, no more, and it rarely received even one-quarter of what it asked; by 1781 the reliance on paper money produced near-bankruptcy; states had varied currency systems of uncertain value, discouraging business and trade. After 1783 there was no longer an army to enforce the law; Congress had no power to enforce treaties. Spain was occupying American territory in West Florida and blocking its trade; Britain refused a treaty of commerce and stayed in possession of the western trading-posts, on the grounds that Loyalists were ill-treated in some states and British debt collections hindered in others; even Barbary pirates seized American ships in the Mediterranean with impunity.

To these constitutional difficulties there was added a severe depression. In the hard winter of 1786 the debt-ridden farmers of Massachusetts, led by Daniel Shays, enraged by heavy taxes and by the hard-money men in Boston, mobbed court-houses and seized weapons. Washington was alarmed by the disorders—"There are combustibles in every State, which a spark might set fire to." "Precedents are dangerous things. Let the reins of government then be braced and held with a steady hand."

Others shared his fears and conclusions. Alexander Hamilton and Noah Webster wrote pamphlets critical of the Articles. All the conservative leaders—Dickinson, Charles Carroll, Robert Morris, Gouverneur Morris, James Wilson—were already advocating a central government, security of trade, power to suppress rebellion, federalism in fact, rather than confederation. Congressional committees had made similar recommendations. There had been proposals for the summoning of a Convention of the People before 1786—one such call had been drafted by Washington in 1783. The Confederation, he thought, was "shadow without substance", "a rope of sand". Washington, in fact, "more than any other man," writes Charles Warren, "was responsible for calling the attention of the people to the defects of the Confederation".[1]

[1] Charles Warren: *The Making of the Constitution* (Boston, 1928), p. 12.

Washington had expressed his views long before. On eleven occasions during the war he had sent identical letters to the Governors of all the states; thirty times he had appealed to those of a particular section. No one knew better than he did the menace of localism, of "contracted ideas, local pursuits and absurd jealousy", as he put it to Knox. His last circular as Commander-in-Chief (June 1783) was an eloquent plea against "relaxing the powers of the Union . . . and exposing us to become the sport of European politics", which would play off one state against another. He went on :

"There are four things which I humbly conceive as essential to the wellbeing, I may even venture to say, to the existence of the United States as an independent power :

1st. An indissoluble Union of the States under One Federal Head.

2dly. A sacred regard to public justice.

3dly. The adoption of a proper peace establishment, and

4thly. The prevalence of that pacific and friendly disposition among the people of the United States which will induce them to forget their local prejudices and policies . . . to sacrifice their individual advantages to the interest of the community."

Nowhere does Washington set forth any coherent theory of government, but, as a result of his experience in the war and in the years of confusion that followed, a consistent political attitude was shaping itself : the need for a "Supreme Power" in government ("influence," he wrote to Henry Lee," is not government. Let us have a government by which our lives, liberties and properties will be secured, or let us know the worst at once"); the importance of commercial interests binding one area to another; admiration for what he, and many others, then mistakenly thought was the "British" plan of a division of government into three equal parts, legislative, executive and judicial; distrust of paper currency, a device of debtors, he thought, to cheat creditors; fear of "faction", of pressure groups among voters, like the Patriotic Societies of the 1780s or the Democratic Societies that sprang up during his own administration, "a kind of *imperium in imperio*", which "as often clog as facilitate public measures"; a Virginian apprehension of the growth of towns and "the tumultuous populace of large cities", whose "indiscriminate violence prostrates . . . all public authority"; faith in land as property; the conviction that a great movement westward was inevitable, that it could not be stopped in 1786 any more than in 1774, that when the western states had numbers, no power could deprive them of the use of the Mississippi; and hope that the continent would become an asylum for "the oppressed and needy of the earth".

There runs throughout Washington's correspondence a strong sense of destiny, a belief that events generate their own energy and that they cannot easily be controlled. He had as a result a distrust of theory, a tempered respect for "the mass of citizens"—"I firmly believe they will always *act well* whenever they can obtain a right understanding of matters"—and a faith in "principal gentlemen", as in war he had a faith in aristocrats for his officers and an unwillingness to fetter them. "To me it appears much wiser and more politic to choose able and honest representatives, and leave them in all national questions to determine from the evidence of reason. . . "

The Mount Vernon Conference of 1785 was followed by a meeting of five states at Annapolis in 1786, which was persuaded by Hamilton and Madison to ask Congress to summon a general convention to Philadelphia to revise the Articles. Congress agreed. All interested observers had hopes of something more than revision—if the Conference failed, said Washington, "there is an end of federal government". Virginia favoured a general revision, and put Washington's name at the head of its list of delegates to the Philadelphia Convention.

He hesitated long before agreeing to go; it was partly a matter of health, partly his distress at the charges against the Society of the Cincinnati, a fraternity of revolutionary veteran officers, who were also to meet in Philadelphia in May. New Englanders—and liberal Southerners like Jefferson—were showing alarm at what they thought its undemocratic and un-American character, and Judge Burke of South Carolina had already called it "a race of hereditary patricians". Washington's first long journey after the war had been to Philadelphia in 1784 to persuade the Society to drop from its rules every possible reference to politics, and these charges strengthened his unwillingness to "intermeddle in public affairs". He was overborne by the persuasions of Knox and Humphreys, of Governor Randolph and of Madison of Virginia. On the 9th May 1787, he set out again on the road to Philadelphia—this time in his carriage. When he entered the city four days later, the guns fired a salute and the bells of Christ Church were rung. On the 25th he was unanimously chosen President of the Convention; was he not, in the view of his fellow-delegate, William Pierce, "like Gustavus Vasa . . . the deliverer of his Country; like Peter the Great . . . the politician and the States-man, and like Cincinnatus"?

Many tributes have been paid to the Constitutional Convention which, in the four months of a Philadelphia summer, transformed the government. It was, said Jefferson, "an assembly of demigods". The scent of incense has increased with the passing of the years, and with justice; a constitution was shaped in 1787 for a farmers' republic of some four million people on the Atlantic coast which has been only occasionally amended, and which still serves, one hundred and seventy years later, as the pattern of government for one hundred and seventy million people spread over a continent. For once profound sectional conflicts were settled by argument, in a convention hall.

Washington was impressed by his fellow-delegates, slow though they were to muster; they were men of affairs, not theorists—Paine, Jefferson and John Adams were in Europe, Sam Adams had not secured election, Patrick Henry "smelt a rat" he said and refused to attend. Four had been his staff officers, thirteen others officers of the Continental Army, another thirteen militia officers; a large proportion were lawyers; many of them were college graduates. They agreed to work in secrecy—an important contribution to their success, even though ultra-democratic outsiders suspected monarchical intrigues.

Had the American people been fully aware of the tensions in the Convention in the first two months, they might well have despaired, as Washington did—he repented "having had any agency in the business". Rhode Island was not represented at all; New Hampshire's delegates came too late. Alexander Hamilton was opposed consistently by his own New York delegation, and it split into fragments. The delegates were at odds on the question of representation from the large and the small states. Though, as President, Washington felt that he should not express opinions on controversial matters, and made only one speech, he supported Randolph's proposals (the Virginia Plan) that representation in both houses of the new National Legislature should be apportioned on the basis of population, that there should be a "National", not a Federal state, and a strong Executive. On some issues he was on the losing side. But debate was not Washington's forte, nor was legislative draftsmanship; his contribution to the shaping of the document was small. Only the blandishments of Benjamin Franklin, the persistence of Madison and Hamilton and the patience of a succession of "grand committees", produced anything like unanimity.

In the end the compromises were worked out—on the form of the judiciary, on the admission of new states, on the complicated but characteristically eighteenth-century device of an Electoral College to select the Executive, on slavery and the slave trade, on the balance between a popularly elected "first branch" of the Legislature and a "second branch" chosen by and representing the separate State Legislatures. A system of checks and balances was designed to restrain all branches—by legislative control of funds, by Presidential veto and by judicial review. If Congress was dominant in matters domestic, the President had greater authority in foreign relations—but no branch of the government could function independently.

The document was finally composed by a Committee on Style, and, after Franklin's moving and wise speech of benediction (read for him by James Wilson), was approved "by the unanimous consent of the States present", though some of the individuals present, like George Mason and Governor Randolph of Virginia, refused to sign. A strong central government was created, with the power to tax and to control foreign relations, its acts binding on the states. The Constitution, Washington thought, was not perfect, but "I sincerely believe it is the best that could be obtained at this time".

Small though his contribution to the drafting of the document might have been, his presence gave authority to the Convention, and his identification with it greatly helped the next stage, which was to win popular support outside Philadelphia. Before the Constitution could come into force it had to secure ratification in nine states, not by their legislatures but by specially summoned conventions. In the campaigns for ratification, it was Washington's name that was the rallying-cry—"the political saviour of America" (the *Worcester Magazine*), or in the *Daily Advertiser* :

> *"Yes, Patriots, by experience taught,*
> *(Their country's guardian-guides)*
> *Concert a plan, with wisdom fraught,*
> *And WASHINGTON presides."*

The battle for ratification is a significant episode in Washington's career, in the growth of the Washington legend and in the history of American partisanship. To many, he was now a hero, the greater because uncrowned; his military record increasingly a matter for hyperbole, his reserve and hesitations increasingly a proof of good democratic diffidence. To the saga of Valley Forge and the triumph of Yorktown, now glowing in retrospect, were added the modesty and the wisdom of a Cincinnatus. Of Washington and Franklin, said the *American Herald,* "the military virtues of the former and the philosophic splendour of the latter will be obscured by the new lustre they will acquire as the legislators of an immense continent".

It was, however, the beginnings of partisanship. The *Connecticut Courant* proposed that those supporting the Constitution, the Federalists, should be called the Washingtonians, and the Anti-Federalists the Shayites. The Anti-Federalist group, hardly yet a party, did not criticise Washington or Franklin directly and in no way impugned their motives, but they suggested that the "unsuspecting goodness and zeal" of the one, in a subject in which he was inexperienced, and the weakness through age of the other, had been used by the "wealthy and ambitious" for their own purposes. Their supporters sprang to their defence in all the states. The Constitution, wrote Knox, was received "with great joy by all the commercial part of the community"; the popularity of the new system was all the greater, hinted

David Humphreys, because of "the universal opinion of your being elected President of the United States". This sentiment was general; Pierce Butler, writing in May 1788, said that the reason for the extensive powers conferred on the President was that the Convention had from the beginning cast Washington for the role, that the office was shaped in fact to match the man.

The fight for ratification, nevertheless, was long and bitter. The Federalists had powerful advocates in key states —Madison in Virginia and Hamilton in New York—but the Anti-Federalists had democratic sentiment on their side, expressed by George Mason, Patrick Henry and Richard Henry Lee in Virginia, Luther Martin in Maryland, and Jefferson writing from Paris. Centralised government, they argued, would destroy state sovereignty; the large states would swamp the smaller; the aristocracy of business or talents would lord it over the lowly-born; titles and the idea of hereditary office had already appeared in the ranks of the Cincinnati; there was inadequate protection of the rights of the individual, of free speech, religious freedom and trial by jury.

Rich little Delaware was the first to ratify, 7th December 1787, but it was not until the following 21st June that the ninth, New Hampshire, did so. Four days later, Virginia ratified, by 89 votes to 79. Washington was not a delegate to the Virginia Convention, and the debate was managed for the Federalists by Madison; but it had been fought in large part on Washington's reputation. "Were it not for one great character in America," said Colonel Grayson on the floor of the Richmond Convention, "so many men would not be for this government."

A month later, New York ratified also, though by three votes only—the work of Hamilton and *The Federalist*. North Carolina in 1789 and Rhode Island in 1790 were forced to conform when the new Congress levied taxes on their exports as though from "foreign" states. The effort to ratify the Constitution had been much more difficult than the writing of the document. It had made clear how strongly felt was the need for a Bill of Rights, and as a result the first ten amendments were added.

Charles Beard has estimated that not more than one-quarter of the adult males voted for delegates to the ratifying conventions and probably not more than one-sixth voted for delegates supporting the Constitution. It was the work of a minority, powerful and property-conscious and no longer revolutionary. Beard goes so far as to claim that since forty of the fifty-five delegates at Philadelphia had interests in Government securities, in slaves or, like Washington, in western land, the Constitution was a device to protect property, not the people, a product of men who feared democracy. Only the Lower House was popularly elected, and its powers were carefully circumscribed; the Senate was the organ of the state legislatures, the Executive was three steps removed from the electorate, the judiciary entirely free from their control. [1]

Beard's view of the Constitution has over the last forty years influenced all writers on the revolutionary period. It is therefore worth emphasising that, though the Founding Fathers were neither disinterested nor popularly selected nor partial to democracy, their judgments were not merely the result of economic pressures. The wealthy states hesitated longest; as Washington commented to Lafayette in a letter in 1788, the opposition to the Constitution came from "the men of large property in the south" not from "the genuine democratical people of the east". The Constitution was in any case as much a lawyers' as a creditors' handiwork;[2] Douglass Adair in an unpublished dissertation at Yale has indicated the intellectual and classical preoccupations of the drafters; Federalism of Washington's type was not a product merely of a self-interest developing after 1783, but was rooted in a fear of political and economic weakness that had been growing for twenty years. Federalism, in fact, was the heir of colonial conservatism.

The Constitution, then, was a bundle of compromises, made workable by men; as Madison later confessed,

[1] C. A. Beard: *An Economic Interpretation of the Constitution of the United States* (Macmillan, New York, 1913). Cf. J. Allen Smith: *The Spirit of American Government* (Macmillan, New York, 1907).
[2] Cf. Schuyler: *The Constitution of the United States* (Macmillan, New York, 1923).

ambiguity was the price of unanimity. It had glaring omissions and weaknesses: what of future territorial acquisitions?; of the regulation of trade and industry?; of political parties, which were not even mentioned?; of citizenship?; of the right of a state to withdraw from the Union? Yet the phrase "We, the people" was something more than a convenient and euphonious fiction. Behind the compromises so carefully contrived there was some sense of national unity.[1] And by common agreement it was embodied in the gentleman-farmer-turned-patriot of Mount Vernon.

This was increasingly the theme throughout 1788. Many critics observed his fifty-sixth birthday with enthusiasm, and the celebration of the 4th July became a general call for Washington for President. A toast was drunk at Wilmington, Delaware, to "Farmer Washington—May he like a second Cincinnatus, be called from the plow to rule a great people". He was pressed from all sides to consider it, but it brought "a kind of gloom upon my mind". His decisions were always made slowly, after much agony of spirit; but there could be little doubt how he would decide: "the good of my country" always triumphed in the end over the "reputation to be put in risk".

There was similarly little doubt over the result of the Presidential elections. Electors were chosen in the different states on the first Wednesday in January 1789, and they met and cast their votes on the first Wednesday in February. Some were chosen by voters, others by the State Legislatures, those of New Jersey by the Governor and Council. Washington was the one name that was nationally known and respected; Hamilton and Madison thought the Vice-President should be a New Englander and recommended John Adams. Washington accepted the suggestion, "the only certain way to prevent the election of an Anti-Federalist". On 4th February, Washington and Adams were chosen for the new offices, the President by unanimous vote.

On the 14th April 1789, Charles Thomson, Secretary of

[1] Cf. W. W. Crosskey: *Politics and the Constitution in the history of the United States*, 2 vols. (University of Chicago Press, 1953); Irving Brant: *James Madison, Father of the Constitution, 1787-1800* (New York, 1950).

Congress, brought the expected summons, and two days later Washington set out from Mount Vernon for another undetermined absence. He promised Congress "only that which can be accomplished by an honest zeal", by "integrity and firmness". He felt, he wrote to Knox, like a culprit "going to his place of execution".

President of the United States

1789–1797

Congress, brought the expected summons, and two days
later Washington set out from Mount Vernon for another
undetermined absence. He promised Congress "only that
which can be accomplished ... that my best zeal", by "integrity
and firmness". He felt, he wrote to Knox, like a culprit
"going to his place of execution".

Chapter Eight

President of the United States
(1789—1797)

WASHINGTON'S journey from Mount Vernon to
New York was a triumphal progress. At Philadelphia
he was greeted by flower-decked maidens and an arch of
victory. At Trenton, "Virgins fair and Matrons grave" welcomed him in song and strewed flowers in his path. As his
barge sailed up the Hudson, it was greeted by sloops on which
choirs sang odes composed for the occasion, one of them tact-
lessly set to the tune of "God Save the King". Such was the
noise of thirteen-gun salutes from ship and shore batteries
that the church bells of New York could not be heard.
Washington took up residence, in a house previously used by
the President of Congress, in Cherry Street—now lost among
the abutments of Brooklyn Bridge.

Washington was inaugurated on 30th April 1789, in a
ceremony in Federal Hall, at the corner of Wall Street. He
wore a suit of brown broadcloth, specially spun in Connecticut, with the buttons carrying the device of a wing-spread
eagle; his stockings were of white silk, his shoe-buckles of
silver; at his side hung a dress-sword; his hair was powdered
and worn in a queue. The oath was administered on the
balcony of the hall, by Chancellor Livingston of New York,
before a vast crowd, and in an atmosphere not only of car-
nival but of dedication. The circumstances of the election,
wrote the New York correspondent of the *Federal Gazette* of
Philadelphia, "the impression of his past services, the con-
course of spectators, the devout fervency with which he
repeated the oath, and the reverential manner in which he
bowed down and kissed the sacred volume—all these con-
spired to render it one of the most august and interesting
spectacles ever exhibited on this globe. It seemed, from the

number of witnesses, to be a solemn appeal to Heaven and earth at once. Upon the subject of this great and Good man, I may perhaps be an enthusiast; but I confess that I was under an awful and religious persuasion that the gracious Ruler of the Universe was looking down at that moment with peculiar complacency. . . ."

The inaugural address was delivered in a low voice; observers noted the awkward gestures now and then, and the restless hands. The President expressed again his strong sense of inadequacy, his "inferior endowments"; he hoped that no local attachments, "separate views nor party animosities" would misdirect the purposes of Congress; he asked that the expenses of his office be met, but he wanted no salary. (In the end Congress decided to pay him a salary of twenty-five thousand dollars per year and to leave him to spend it as he pleased.) It was not an orator's effort, and there were critics of the fumbling delivery, but the awkwardness was further evidence of the man's sincerity and won sympathy. Fisher Ames, a judge of public speeches, sat, he said, "entranced"— Washington's "aspect grave, almost to sadness; his modesty, actually shaking" seeming "an allegory in which virtue was personified". The French Minister went further : the President had "the soul, look and figure of a hero united in him".

He did not find it difficult to become the part. His natural dignity of manner was now enhanced by age—"Time has made havoc upon his face," said Ames. And Washington sensed the value to an unformed nation of some measure of pomp and circumstance. It does not seem to be true that he wanted to be called "His Mightiness, the President of the United States and Protector of their Liberties"; a letter to David Stuart echoes what his experience with the Cincinnati had proved—that titles were apt to arouse resentment. The Senate favoured "His Highness", and "His Elective Majesty" and "His Excellency" were proposed, but the House decided to use merely the simple title "The President of the United States".

Yet there was considerable formality. There were fourteen white servants and seven slaves in the house on Cherry Street, and then in the Macomb House on Broadway, to which he moved in 1790. At his wife's Friday evening levees Washington's deportment was "invariably grave"; there were no handshakes, but formal bows; remarks were brief, and the President withdrew at 9 p.m. He used a canary-coloured chariot imported from England, decorated with gilded nymphs and cupids and his own coat-of-arms. It was drawn on formal occasions by six cream horses. This was again less a case of the man adapting himself to the office as of the office reflecting the character and dignity of the man and the tastes of a successful planter. Martha, who joined him in May and was "Lady Washington" to all the world, did not take to it so easily—"I lead a very dull life here . . . I never goe to any public place. . . . I am more like a state prisoner than anything else, there is certain bounds set for me which I must not depart from—and as I cannot doe as I like I am obstinate and stay at home a great deal."

Washington spent eighteen months in New York, organizing a government. He inherited from the Confederation only a handful of unpaid clerks and a large number of debts. North Carolina and Rhode Island were not yet in the Union; Vermont was still intriguing with Canada; Britain held on to the western posts and was dangerously friendly with the Indians—and in 1790, against the possibility of war with Spain, she sought permission in advance from the United States to move troops through the western territory. The American Army had 840 officers and men; there was no navy at all. Hamilton thought the Constitution "frail and worthless"; his opinion seemed nearer reality than Washington's talk of a "hopeful experiment".

Washington was on, he knew, "untrodden ground"; everything he did would set a precedent. What distinguished his work in creating the administrative system was his sense of order, his discretion and his freedom from advocacy. What he wrote to his favourite nephew, Bushrod Washington, in refusing his application for appointment as United States District Attorney for Virginia, held of his attitude generally : "My political conduct in nominations, even if I was uninfluenced by principle, must be exceedingly circumspect and proof against just criticism, for the eyes of Argus are upon me." He regarded the executive branch as distinct from but equal to the Legislature; the choice and form of legislation was a matter for Congress, but the President had the right to remove and, subject to Congressional endorsement, to appoint officials. This was not an easy task; there were some three thousand applications for Federal employment even before a single job was created. The effect was that control of administrative and diplomatic officials fell to the Executive, not Congress.

One of the first products of the new Establishment was a judiciary, "the firmest pillar of good government". The Constitution had provided only for a Supreme Court; the Judiciary Act of 1789 set up the system of which the basic features are still in operation—district courts, circuit courts of appeal and a Supreme Court of one Chief Justice and of five (now eight) Associates. To ensure uniform legal interpretations throughout the nation, the Supreme Court was to rule on the constitutionality of state court decisions. John Jay was appointed Chief Justice, and the Court sat for the first time in February 1790, resplendent in judicial robes but without the white wigs of their English counterparts.

Treaty making was a more difficult matter. Washington took quite literally the Constitutional provision that treaties be made with "the advice and consent" of the Senate. He thought that on some occasions it should be possible for the President to appear before the Senate, to explain the purpose of a treaty and to obtain forthwith a "yes" or "no" on the points he raised. In order to settle the long-standing boundary dispute between the Creek Indians and the State of Georgia, Washington proposed negotiations with the Creeks, to attempt to wean them from the temptations of an alliance with the Spanish in Louisiana. In August 1789, with this in mind, he appeared before the Senate in person with a series of proposals. The most vigorous dissenter from them among the Senators, William Maclay, asked that the treaty be deferred to a committee. According to Maclay, whose portraits were often etched with acid, Washington stalked out with a "discontented air", declaring that deferment "defeats every purpose of my coming here". He got the Senate's approval two days later, but the incident had important consequences : it became the rule for treaties to be presented to the Senate for approval after, and not before, they were negotiated; in the Senate the committee system began to develop; and the Senate made it clear that in its own estimation it was not a

Council of State but a legislative body, in no way subordinate to the President.

Congress established three executive departments—State, Treasury and War. It was, however, Washington's wish to obtain advice from his aides before making decisions that gradually made of these officials an American Cabinet. They were responsible to the President only, not to Congress, and they became the originators of the policy of the Administration; they were all consulted on all matters, not merely on their specialisms. The Cabinet, unmentioned in the Constitution, thus became a privy council, which the Founding Fathers had clearly meant the Senate to be.

To the State Department, Washington appointed Thomas Jefferson, a forty-six-year-old fellow-Virginian whose path so far had rarely crossed his own and who had just completed five years as the United States Minister to France. Hamilton, thirty-two years old and his war-time secretary, with his ambition greater than ever as a result of his marriage to the daughter of General Schuyler, became Secretary of the Treasury. Henry Knox, Washington's corpulent old Chief of Artillery, continued as Secretary of War, an office he had held under the Confederation. Edmund Randolph, former Governor of Virginia and for a time critic of the Constitution, became Attorney-General.

While Hamilton was becoming familiar with his task—Jefferson did not arrive in New York until March 1790—Washington undertook in October and November 1789 a tour of New England, going as far north as Portsmouth, and returning, as John Trumbull remarked, "all fragrant with the odour of incense". His *Diaries* contain some revealing glimpses of his Northern tour. He compelled gouty Governor Hancock of Massachusetts, his old rival for the post of Commander-in-Chief in 1775, to pay his respects to the President, and not vice versa. Pleased by the kindness shown him in a humble home near Uxbridge, Massachusetts, he sent presents to the daughter of the house—"As I do not give these things with a view to have it talked of, or even to its being known, the less there is said about the matter the better you will please me." He had some dull days in Connecticut:

"It being contrary to law and disagreeable to the People of this State to travel on the Sabbath day—and my horses, after passing through such intolerable roads, wanting rest, I stayed at Perkins' tavern (which, by the bye, is not a good one) all day—and a meeting-house being within a few rods of the door, I attended morning and evening service, and heard very lame discourses from a Mr. Pond.''

On his return, he issued a proclamation that 26 November 1789 should be a Day of Thanksgiving. These activities strengthened the sense of national unity. The only criticism they evoked was an occasional mild protest in New England at the degree of ceremony that appeared to hedge a President.

It was another matter with the nationally inspired financial programme of his first lieutenant. That programme gave energy and direction to the government, and made its author the driving spirit, in some ways the prime minister, of the Administration. But it heralded controversy. The three great state papers of Alexander Hamilton were his reports on *Publick Credit* (January 1790), on *A National Bank* (December 1790) and on *Manufactures* (December 1791). The first of these did not cause but further widened differences already apparent between Federalists and Anti-Federalists, between what Maclay called the party, on the one hand, of the speculators and the courtiers ("the party of interest"), and, on the other, "the party of principle". But Hamilton, if a courtier, had his own principles in abundance, even if the most avowed of them was the advancement of their author.

Hamilton was convinced that the efficiency of the newly created Federal Government depended, first, on energy in the Executive branch—on what he called "Executive impulse", and second, in no way inferior, on the establishment of sound public credit. He urged that all outstanding foreign and domestic debts incurred by the states or by Congress be assumed and paid by the Federal Government. This would serve a political as well as an economic purpose; it would impress foreign governments and would bind creditors to the national cause; "a public debt", he argued, "is a public blessing". Of illegitimate birth in the West Indies, he became the great protagonist of birth and connection. Of poor origins, he believed that government was the preserve of "the rich and the well-born", that man's prevailing passions "are ambition and interest". Nor did he hide his contempt for democracy—"your people, Sir, is a great beast". He proposed that a Bank of the United States should be established, and that a system of tariff duties and excises should be used to provide revenue. His proposals have been the core of that Federalist economic programme that, later, Whigs and, later still, Republicans have made their own.

Despite the appeal of these measures to commercial and financial interests, they were far from popular. Suspicious Congressmen like Madison and crotchety Senators like Maclay objected to paying off the domestic debt of the Confederation at face value to bond-holders who were often merely speculators. Madison argued that Federal assumption of state debts did injustice to those states, mainly Southern, that had already done their duty by their creditors but that would now be called upon to contribute to those states, mainly Northern, that had not. In any event, assumption would strengthen the Federal government and would weaken the states. Patrick Henry argued with customary vehemence that the Constitution gave no authority to the Federal Government to assume the obligations of the states. On the bank and excise questions South and North were in opposing camps, the South against, the North for them.

The debate on these issues was not confined to Congress. If Fenno's *Gazette of the United States* became the Hamiltonian vehicle, critics appeared in the pages of the *New-York Journal* and of the *Pennsylvania Gazette* :

> *"Each day a fresh report he broaches,*
> *That Spies and Jews may ride in coaches,*
> *Soldiers and farmers, don't despair,*
> *Untaxed as yet are Earth and Air."*

In the debate on the assumption of state debts, Congress was evenly divided, and Washington was determined to remain above the battle. At its height, in May 1790, he was seriously ill with pneumonia and feared likely to die. This was his second illness within a year, and his recovery was slow. The thought of a convalescence at Mount Vernon when Congress recessed became more attractive than ever.

By the time Congress rose, it had found an answer to its deadlock on the assumption of the state debts. Jefferson, recently arrived from Paris, brought pressure on his Southern friends to support assumption on condition that the Federal Government should ultimately be sited on the Potomac. Robert Morris was also a party to the deal, and it was agreed that Philadelphia should become the temporary seat of government—no doubt he had hopes of its becoming permanent.

After a decade in Philadelphia (1790–1800) the "Federal City" was to be built near Georgetown on the Potomac. This compromise, though vaunted by later historians, was a matter of much bitterness at the time. Jefferson later claimed, not entirely convincingly, that he did not appreciate all that was involved in the deal, that he had not wanted to provide "pabulum for stock-jobbers". New Yorkers were indignant, and the *New-York Journal* charged that "Miss Assumption" had given birth to two illegitimate children "Philadelphia" and "Potowmacus", as a result of the seductive promises of "Mr. Residence". More sensitive New Englanders were glad to move away from Manhattan's dram-shops. Pennsylvanians were angry at the idea of an artificial capital being built in a muddy and mosquito-ridden swamp in preference to the facilities of Philadelphia (the only city at that time with paved streets and a rudimentary water-supply). Their testy junior Senator saw a conspiracy on the part of the President, "who pushes the Potomac". "The President has become in the hands of Hamilton, the dish-clout of every dirty speculation, as his name goes to wipe away blame and silence all murmuring."

The charges would soon grow more savage than this, but there is no evidence that Washington sought to influence Congress in any way on the choice of site. On the contrary; on visiting Rhode Island in August, in order to welcome it into the Union, he was seeing his task more than ever as a national one. "We must drive far away the daemon of party spirit and local reproach." No doubt he was privately happy at the thought of a Federal City within range, even perhaps within sight, of his own broad acres, though he was not to live to see it. In September 1790, the capital was transferred to Philadelphia, and for two months the President was able to revisit Mount Vernon.

The first two years of the Administration were years of unusual harmony. The country was prosperous. The site of

the new Federal City was agreed upon, L'Enfant was drawing his grandiose plans and Commissioners had been appointed to superintend the work. The anniversary of the
President's birthday, 22nd February 1791, was treated as a
national festival.

The President was as concerned to see the various sections
of the country as he was to establish a unifying government
and the public credit. Having visited the North in 1789-90,
he spent two months in 1791 on a Southern journey—
through the sandy roads of the Carolina pine barrens, thin in
population and in soil, to Charleston and Savannah, returning by way of Augusta and Guilford and the scene of the
Southern battles—"a Journey of 1,887 miles . . . without
meeting with any interruption".

His diary of the Southern tour is unusually full and frank,
and reflects not only physical but social endurance. In
Charleston, which he had not seen before, he spent a week;
during that time he held three receptions, attended two
breakfasts, ate seven formal dinners, listened and replied to
four addresses, attended two assemblies and a concert, visited
the sites of the sieges and drank sixty toasts. He enjoyed particularly the "elegant dancing" of Southern ladies, "respectable" and "superbly dressed", wearing ribbons or bandeaux
that carried sentimental tributes to him.

He was gratified by the evidence of his own popularity,
but even more by the discovery that the country was in an
"improving state". There were problems ahead—"the direful
effect of slavery", careless farming and sterility of soil which
would in a few years drive people west. But "tranquility
reigns among the people with that disposition towards the
general government which is likely to preserve it. They begin
to feel the good effects of equal laws and equal protection."

Yet 1791 brought problems to try the domestic peace.
France was now in the throes of revolution and faced a slave
rebellion in Santo Domingo, her richest West Indian possession. Washington promised all possible help to France in the
Caribbean, meanwhile expressing to Lafayette, now grown
into a leading personality in Paris, the hope that a government might emerge in France that would be "respectfully
energetic and founded on the broad basis of liberality and
the rights of man". The temper and situation of France

might, however, push Britain and Spain into alliance. It might even involve a request by France that the United States fulfil the terms of the military alliance of 1778. A war might break out among the powers of Europe that could imperil American frontiers. From these political disputes Washington hoped to stay aloof; what distance of itself did not do might be helped by "a conduct of circumspection, moderation and forbearance". And there were signs that this conduct was bringing dividends. Relations with Britain seemed more cordial with the arrival in October 1791 of George Hammond as British Minister—the first British diplomatic agent formally accredited to America.

Whatever she might be in Philadelphia, however, in the Ohio country Britain was still a frontier ally of the Indians, and these were an immediate and not a contingent problem. The attempt to settle the persistent troubles of Georgia with Choctaw, Creek and Cherokee had led Washington, in 1790, to invite the Creek chiefs to New York. Their leader, the colourful half-breed Alexander McGillivray, signed a treaty in which the Creek tribes were guaranteed their hunting-grounds. The chiefs were dined and fêted by the Tammany Society, and Washington believed—optimistically, as it proved—that the treaty had brought peace to the south-western border. In the North-West the situation remained uglier, with Britain, not Spain, in connivance. The Miami and Wabash tribes had raided in Ohio and Kentucky, and General Harmar's punitive column, based on Fort Washington in Ohio (the present Cincinnati), had failed to curb them. "I expected *little*", said Washington, "from the moment I heard he was a *drunkard*." In 1790 General St. Clair had been instructed to establish a strong military post in the North-West, at Miami Village (the present Fort Wayne). Treaties were to be attempted with the tribes that seemed well-disposed, but St. Clair was to "seek the enemy". Jefferson agreed—the Indians must be given "a thorough drubbing".

The event was a repetition of Braddock's disaster on the Monongahela : fifteen miles from his goal, St. Clair was attacked and overwhelmed, and nearly one thousand of his force were casualties. The legend has grown that the news of the disaster reached Washington during one of Mrs. Washington's Friday levees, that he concealed his feelings until the guests had gone, and that then a storm broke in the Morris house like that that had struck St. Clair. In fact, the newspapers had carried plausible reports of the disaster for a day or two beforehand, and the dispatches from St. Clair were addressed not to the President but to the Secretary of War. The President can hardly have been unprepared for the disaster. Congress was promptly and fully informed, and a new force was raised, with Anthony Wayne at its head. Though a sense of alarm swept through the West and with it a mounting nationalism, there were no political repercussions.

By the end of 1791, however, political partisanship was being generated in domestic matters. In November 1791, Fisher Ames wrote that "tranquility has smoothed the surface" but that "faction glows within like a coalpit". It was not merely a clash of political philosophy, of Hamilton *versus* Jefferson, or of the discussions for or against assumption, the excise tax and the Bank proposals. There was still a widespread fear of centralised government—"I do not believe," said Ames, "that the hatred of the Jacobites towards the House of Hanover was ever more deadly than that which is borne by many of the partisans of State power towards the government of the United States." The fiscal policy of the government and the preferred position of the Bank of the United States were believed by many to be responsible for the speculative mania of 1791. The *National Gazette* campaigned against the excise tax and against what it thought the unconstitutionality of the Hamiltonian programme. "The free citizens of America will not quietly suffer the well-born few to trample them under foot." "Another revolution must and will be brought about in favour of the people."

These differences, though not limited to, were most acute inside the Administration. They had emerged first in August 1790 when the Cabinet had discussed American policy in the event of a British war with Spain and of a British attempt to conquer Louisiana and the Floridas. To avert this, Jefferson was ready for war with Britain; his colleagues would not go beyond remonstrance. The differences became clearer on the assumption question and on the constitutionality of the Bank. Washington was particularly embarrassed by the conflicting views on this last question, for Jefferson, Madison and Attorney-General Randolph denied that Congress had the right to establish such a corporation. Hamilton took the view that anything could be done so long as it was not expressly forbidden by the Constitution. As with the drafting of the document, so with the interpretation, Washington favoured strength and authority at the centre, and this took him into the Hamiltonian camp; he signed the Bill establishing the Bank in February 1791. Yet he was fully sympathetic to Jefferson's warning—"if the pro and con hang so even as to balance his [the President's] judgment, a just respect for the wisdom of the Legislature would naturally decide the balance in favour of their opinion". He was careful to honour this advice, and indeed to follow Hamilton's own insistence that "it is always best for the chief magistrate to be as little implicated as possible in the specific approbation of a particular measure proceeding from a particular officer".

This was proving increasingly difficult in a team in which, as Oliver Wolcott put it (October 1791)—"The principles of dissension exist, but the principles are the merest trifles." "Mr. H. and Mr. J." he found, were ready to quarrel over most matters, especially whether "Tom Paine or Edmund Burke are the greatest fools". Jefferson was a frank admirer of Paine's *Rights of Man*, which was dedicated to Washington. To Jefferson, as to Paine, the French Revolution and the American were closely linked, and he was suspicious of what he thought Hamilton's over-frank admiration of the British constitution. He gave a post as translator in the State Department to Philip Freneau, who proceeded to edit the *National Gazette*, and to make of it a journal increasingly critical of the Federalists.

Despite Wolcott's warnings, Washington tried to regard this conflict as one of principle rather than of personality—a view it was increasingly hard to maintain. He did not think in personal terms, and could not conceive of anything being more important than the establishment of the government on firm foundations. Once it was established, it was to be "a government of accommodation as well as a government of laws". The clash was alarming, because it was echoed in some of the states and in Congress, and because it suggested a geographical division on policy between North and South. Washington himself was not involved in the conflict, and only indirectly in the public charges and counter-charges. Nevertheless, the prospect of retirement in March 1793 became ever more attractive.

This mood of hesitation, though familiar, seems by 1792 to have been something more than gentlemanly affectation. Washington was growing deaf, and his memory, he said, was beginning to fail him. There is little evidence for this where Mount Vernon is concerned—in the winter of 1792-3 he wrote twenty-one letters to his manager at Mount Vernon, of which the first ran to some three thousand words, and they all showed a minute knowledge of its affairs. In the spring of 1792, however, he had had a number of discussions with Madison on the shape of a farewell address. He found him a convinced opponent of the idea of retirement : the rise of party spirit was a reason rather for staying on, than for withdrawing; another four years would save the country from the risks of a new regime or the dangers of monarchy, and would give "tone and firmness". Hamilton, Knox and Randolph endorsed this advice. Jefferson's original assumption was that the President's mind was made up—"I knew we were some day to try to walk alone, and if the essay should be made while you should be alive and looking on, we should derive confidence from that circumstance, and resource, if it failed." But in the summer of 1792 Jefferson, too, was urging Washington to consent to serve again, and used an argument that had influence—"North and South will hang together if they have you to hang on."

The summer was full of rumours : of Indian troubles, of the arrival in New Orleans of five regiments of Spanish troops, of the formation of a Jacobin club in Philadelphia, of efforts in Pennsylvania to obstruct the excise laws. These tensions brought the factional clash into the open. In May Jefferson had listed a series of charges against the Secretary of the Treasury. Washington drew these up under twenty-one headings and invited Hamilton's comments, "to obtain light and to pursue truth". The reply ran to fourteen thousand words; Hamilton admitted that speculation in government securities had had some bad effects on those engaged in it, but denied that a single member of Congress could "properly" he called a stock-jobber. For the rest, there was a complete refutation of all the charges.

To both men Washington appealed for compromise and moderation, for "liberal allowances, mutual forbearances and temporising yieldings", instead of "wounding suspicions and irritable charges". He appealed in vain. Jefferson thought Hamilton's principles were "adverse to liberty" and that he was exerting a dangerous influence over the Legislature. Hamilton charged Jefferson with "whispers and insinuations". But both agreed that Washington was indispensable, "the only man in the United States who possessed the confidence of the whole . . . no other person . . . would be thought anything more than the head of a party".

When the time came for his Annual Message to Congress in November 1792—the date he had suggested to Madison, months before, as appropriate for a farewell message—Washington said nothing of his intention to resign. Though later letters suggest that he had not yet finally closed the door on the possibility, failure then to announce withdrawal made his re-election certain. By that time the states were preparing to name electors. The party battle was transferred to the Vice-Presidency. When the votes were counted, 13th February 1793, Washington was again unanimously chosen; Adams was re-elected to the Vice-Presidency with seventy-seven votes against fifty for Hamilton's rival in New York politics, George Clinton. And Virginia's entire electoral vote of twenty-one had gone to the New Yorker. This, seeming a paradox, was to be a portent. The alliance of rural South and urban North was to become the nucleus of the Jeffersonian party. The Senate, not yet established as the senior chamber, remained Federalist, but there was an Anti-Federalist, Republican or "Democratick" majority—the terms were interchangeable and pejorative—in the Lower House. There were other portents in 1793; despite the unanimous choice for President, Freneau's paper had begun to train its guns not only on the Cabinet but on its Head, to sneer at "the drawing Room", "those apparent trifles, birthday odes" and the Friday evening levees. There was a certain symbolism in the fact that on 18th September 1793 Washington laid the cornerstone of the Federal Capitol; in four years the foundations had been laid, but an uglier term lay ahead.

On 4th March 1793, Washington was inaugurated President for a second time. Already the European scene was darker: Louis XVI was guillotined in January; on 1st February, France declared war on Britain and a great European coalition was formed to resist the Revolution. This situation made explicit what had hitherto been implicit in Washington's attitude. When the French Revolution broke out in 1789, the fact on which he seized was American remoteness. "We, at this great distance . . . hear of wars and rumours of wars, as if they were the events or reports of another planet." At times, particularly in his letters to Lafayette, he expressed sympathy with the Revolution, and he received from the Marquis a picture of the captured Bastille, with the main key of the fortress—"a tribute, which I owe as a son to my adopted father, as an aid-de-camp to my general, as a missionary of liberty to its patriarch". In acknowledging the gift, Washington referred to the key as a "token of victory gained by liberty over despotism".

Yet to Lafayette he could also be frank in avowing the threats to America presented by a war in Europe. He wanted, he wrote in 1790, to be "unentangled in the crooked policies of Europe", and sought only the free navigation of the Mississippi. He sensed the tumult and the paroxysms of France, the "more haste than good speed in their innovations", and wanted no part in the attendant political disputes of Europe. These views were reinforced by the events of 1790–3, domestic as well as foreign, and by the alarms in Florida and New Orleans, in the Caribbean and in the Ohio country.

With the declaration of war by France on Britain in 1793, the United States issued a proclamation (April) declaring her intention to pursue "a conduct friendly and impartial towards the belligerent powers". It was drawn up by Randolph, and it did not contain the word "neutrality". This proclamation marks the real beginning of the break between President and Secretary of State. For Washington it was an expression of neutrality, in fact if not in word. Jefferson's view was more devious. Publicly, he argued that by holding back a declaration of neutrality, the United States might induce the European powers to bid for it, and thus secure "the broadest privileges of neutral nations". Privately, however, he thought it pusillanimous, a "milk-and-water" instrument, which disregarded American obligations both to the cause of France under the alliance of 1778 and to the larger cause of liberty. When "Pacificus" Hamilton came out in support of the proclamation, Jefferson encouraged "Helvidius" Madison to attack him—"For God's sake, my dear Sir, take up your pen, select the most striking heresies and cut him to pieces in the face of the public." However much idealism lay behind Jefferson's methods, they appear less noble and infinitely less discreet than Washington's.

Washington was convinced of the wisdom of neutrality. His purpose, he later declared to Henry, was "to keep the United States free from political connections with *every* other country, to see them independent of all and under the influence of none. In a word, I want an *American* character, that the powers of Europe may be convinced we act for *ourselves* and not for *others*".

He admitted a friendship for, even some obligation towards, Lafayette, and requested Gouverneur Morris, the American Minister in Paris, to convey informally to the French the regard of all Americans for him; but when Henry Lee informed Washington that he was considering enlistment in the French Army, and requested advice, the reply was impeccable and magisterial:

"As a public character, I can say *nothing* on the subject. . . . As a private man, I am unwilling to say much. Give advice I shall not. All I can do, then . . . is to declare that if the case which you have suggested was mine, I should ponder well before I resolved, not only for private considerations, but on public grounds."

And then, just to be sure, he advised Lee to burn the letter. If Lee failed to act on one piece of advice, he saw the point, however guarded, of the other.

The problems posed by the war in Europe were not just matters of personal alignment and personal sympathy. Some three-quarters of America's trade was with Britain, and 90 per cent. of her imports came from Britain. New England favoured Britain, therefore, as surely as southern agrarians did not. But it was still hard for the friends of Britain in America to raise their voices; Britain on the seas and in the Western posts was still an arrogant power.

The first real challenge to the Federalist quest for neutrality was presented, however, by the arrival of Edmund Charles Genêt as the French Girondin Minister to the United States. France could hardly have selected a more tactless ambassador—a man, Gouverneur Morris warned Washington, with "more of genius than ability", with "at first blush the manner and look of an upstart". As luck would have it, his ship was blown out of its course, and he landed, in April 1793, at Charleston, in "Democratick" territory. His twenty-eight-day journey, by easy stages, to Philadelphia, was a procession which evoked an enthusiasm reminiscent of the President's own, four years before. It gave him a quite false notion of his popularity and of his role. Genêt was deterred neither by the announcement of neutrality nor by a chilly reception from Washington in Philadelphia. He saw himself, apparently, as the Minister, not of a government to a government, but of a people to a people. With the support of the Jeffersonians, he proceeded to act in most undiplomatic fashion. As he lyrically reported to his changing masters in Paris—"I provision the Antilles, I excite the Canadians to free themselves from the yoke of England, I arm the Kentuckians." He organised expeditions against Florida and Louisiana—George Rogers Clark found himself "Commander-in-chief of the French Revolutionary Legion on the Mississippi River". He sent out privateers and he sponsored Jacobin clubs.

By June, even Jefferson was alarmed at this—"indefensible"; "never was so calamitous an appointment made; hotheaded, all imagination, no judgment, passionate". By August he was, thought Jefferson, "absolutely incorrigible", and the Cabinet unanimously demanded his recall. The responsibility, however, was not Genêt's alone, but Jefferson's, who had at first abetted his schemes.

By 1793 Madison and Jefferson were becoming afraid that behind the mask of neutrality lay "a secret Anglomanny". Jefferson's five years in Paris had left him with no love of the English—"those rich, proud, hectoring, swearing, squibbling, carnivorous animals who live on the other side of the Channel"—or of those in America who admired their institutions or imitated their ways. And though his own naïveté made him an easy victim, Genêt became the instrument of

Jefferson's policy. Four years later, he accused Jefferson of encouraging him and of persuading him that Washington, "that excellent man", was "controlled by the English". He also charged Jefferson with denouncing him to "Robertspierre", and said that had he attempted to return to Paris he would certainly have been executed. He expressed his thanks to Washington for saving him from this fate. Another fate awaited him. In the phrase of Professor Bailey, "hand in hand with the daughter of Governor Clinton, he faced the altar instead of the guillotine", and died, appropriately enough, on Bastille Day, 14th July 1834.

Washington was kind to Genêt, but resolute in his neutrality. He believed that "the defensive alliance" with France had ended with the treaty of peace with Britain in 1783. His first obligation was to the United States, and to the facts of a revolution in Europe from which, if possible, the United States must be protected. He told Congress :

"There is a rank due to the United States among nations, which will be withheld, if not absolutely lost, by the reputation of weakness. If we desire to avoid insult, we must be able to repel it; if we desire to secure peace, one of the most powerful instruments of our rising prosperity, it must be known that we are at all times ready for War."

The affaire Genêt added zest to the domestic party battle.

Years later, in correspondence with Jefferson and with memory blurred, Adams wrote of the "thousands" in the Philadelphia mobs who threatened to drag Washington from his house and to overturn the government. He was convinced that revolution was averted only by the coming to Philadelphia in the late summer of a still more deadly scourge—yellow fever. Out of a population of some 45,000, 4,000 died. Hamilton was stricken, but, aided by his remarkable vitality, survived. Washington, like other members of the Administration, spent part of the period away from the city. He returned from Mount Vernon as the weather grew cold. The political temperature stayed high. The Marseillaise and "Ça Ira" were now the marching songs of Anti-Federalism. To the Jeffersonians the Federalists were "British boot-lickers", and some of their editors, like Callender and Duane, had choicer epithets. The Democratic Societies or Jacobin Clubs, the *National Gazette* and the *Philadelphia Aurora* were now the instruments of a party, of which Jefferson was clearly becoming the leader. To Fenno and Cobbett and the Federalist *Gazette of the United States*, the Republicans were "Democraticks", "filthy Jacobins", "frog-eating, man-eating, blood-drinking cannibals".

Believing in the soundness of the new American institutions that were now repeatedly being attacked, convinced of the importance of neutrality towards and aloofness from revolutionary Europe, distrustful not only of revolutionary doctrines but of any theory that was joined to fanaticism and sophistry, Washington's idea of good government was by 1794 almost identical with Hamilton's. The identity was never complete; Hamilton was bolder and brasher than Washington, with a gift of words and a grasp of finance—and of intrigue—far surpassing the President's. Washington, though less intellectual, was infinitely superior to Hamilton in judgment. Jefferson's range was wider than either of theirs, his cast of mind more contemplative and contradictory. But Washington could have little sympathy with Jeffersonian ideas; and the man of affairs found himself much more attuned to the administrative emphasis and to the concrete programme of the Hamiltonians. From 1789 to 1794 he was above party, an enemy of what he called "faction", a Federalist. By 1794 he went further and became a Hamiltonian. The partisanship spread. Madison went the other way, and Jefferson resigned the Secretaryship of State on 31st December 1793, to be replaced by Edmund Randolph.

It was therefore with alarm that Washington viewed the so-called Whisky Rebellion of 1794. The excise tax was a heavy burden on the western farmers, who, unable to transport their corn and rye across the Alleghenies or down the Mississippi, converted it into whisky. Every farmer in the back-country manufactured it. In 1794 open rebellion against the excise tax broke out among the farmers of western Pennsylvania, and Federal Treasury officials, like state officials before them, were driven back. Under Hamilton's persuasions, Washington saw in the rebellion "the first *formidable* fruit" of the Democratic Societies, and of "their diabolical leader, Genêt". Unless it were broken, "we may bid adieu to all government in this country, except mob and club government".

There were no federal police to enforce the law, but the Constitution empowered the Federal Government to call out the state militia when necessary. But would the states acknowledge this authority? Washington put the matter to the test, called out the militia, and talked of leading it in person over the mountains. Hamilton accompanied the troops as a kind of political commissar. By the time the militia appeared—and 15,000 turned out at the call—the rebellion had come to an end. Having displayed the power of the Federal Government—and satisfied conservative opinion as much as he alarmed Jeffersonians—the President, in July 1795, pardoned the insurgents. For him firmness again was allied to clemency. Hamilton's prestige was more seriously affected; when he played the double role of man on horseback and Grand Inquisitor, he became more than ever the butt of the Jeffersonians.

The same Hamiltonian policy led Washington to attempt a settlement of the disputes with Britain. Anthony Wayne's victory over the Indians at Fallen Timbers in 1794 opened up the Ohio country and weakened British influence over her forest allies. But Britain still held the fur-posts, still excluded American ships from her West Indian ports and still dickered over the boundary with Maine. She was countering the revived and lucrative American trade with the French West Indies by invoking the Rule of 1756 (that trade closed in time of peace could not be opened in time of war) and, under its cloak, seizing American ships. She claimed the right also to search American ships for British deserters at a time of lax naturalisation laws and inadequate proof of citizenship. This interference was particularly resented in New England, the Federalist stronghold, and in the debates in the House of Representatives in 1794 New England and the Middle States seemed in process of aligning on this issue with the South. Despite the unpopularity of any suggestion of rapprochement with Britain, Washington felt that an effort should be made to settle these outstanding problems, and that it should be done by a special mission and a treaty requiring only Cabinet and Senate approval. Accordingly, in April 1794 he dispatched John Jay as special envoy to London. Not the least important of Jay's discoveries, so he wrote to Washington, was that "No other man enjoys so completely the esteem and confidence of this nation as you do; nor, except the King, is any one so popular."

When the news of the Treaty signed by Jay (November 1794) reached the United States in the following March, Washington's popularity at home was given its severest test. Jay knew that his work would meet with opposition, but thought that the terms were the best that could be obtained : Britain agreed to evacuate the fur posts by 1796, and to open her East Indian ports to American ships; she agreed to open her West Indian ports also, but only to vessels under seventy tons; the United States agreed not to export sugar, molasses, coffee, cotton or cocoa; joint commissions were to settle the Maine boundary dispute and claims for damages arising from seizures, but nothing was said about impressment, the trade of neutrals with France or about Indians. Washington did not pretend to like these terms, and kept the Treaty for three months before submitting it to the Senate. The Senate ratified the treaty after long discussions, in June 1795, by the minimum number of votes necessary, but rejected the West Indian clauses and the ban on exports.

When the terms of the treaty leaked to the Press, they met a wave of popular protest. "The cry against the Treaty," Washington wrote to Hamilton, "is like that against a mad-dog; and every one, in a manner, seemed engaged on running it down." There was worse than this waiting for Hamilton, whose support for the Treaty led to his being stoned in the streets. A placard appeared : "D—— John Jay ! D—— every one who won't d—— John Jay ! D—— every one who won't put lights in his windows and sit up all night d——ing John Jay !" For a time the House refused to appropriate the money called for by the Treaty and requested a copy of Jay's instructions. Washington refused—"The nature of foreign negotiations requires caution, and their success must often depend upon secrecy." This was, he claimed, the reason for vesting the treaty-making power in the President, acting with the advice and consent of the Senate. Washington saw the dispute not as one on the merits of the Treaty alone, but on the treaty-making power and the Constitution itself. It was only "the Colossus of the President's merits with the people", wrote Jefferson, that had allowed the "Anglo-men" to get their handiwork enacted, after months of wrangling. The President signed the Treaty in August 1795. Though the Treaty of 1795 failed to make clear what were the rights of neutrals and he had his reservations about it, Washington was right in thinking that it was the best treaty that could be won at the time. It represented, on however small a scale, the beginnings of arbitration in Anglo-American disputes. Spain became so alarmed at the prospect of a closer Anglo-American accord that she proceeded to negotiate a settlement of her own disputes with the United States in the Godoy-Pinckney Treaty, or the Treaty of San Lorenzo, signed in the shadow of that Escorial Palace that symbolised the power of a now fading empire.

This Treaty got little attention and less applause, but it was a complete diplomatic success for Pinckney : Spain granted to the United States the rights of navigation on the Mississippi and the right of deposit at New Orleans free of duty for ocean-going American goods; she recognised the thirty-first parallel as the northern boundary of Florida and agreed to try to restrain the Indians from border raids. The Treaty helped the United States to retain the fluctuating loyalty of the Kentucky and Tennessee area, now becoming states, it pointed the way South and West, and for a generation it made the nation Mississippi-minded. The President who had forty years before marched into the then West and seen its potentialities, and who twenty years before had considered retreating over the Alleghenies with his weary and dwindling forces, had good reason for satisfaction with the settlement of 1795.

By 1795 the domestic scene, however, had become completely partisan. Randolph, who had succeeded Jefferson as Secretary of State in 1793, was dismissed in 1795 on the doubtful grounds of receiving bribes from France. Washington was angered by what he thought the intrigues of one whom he had always befriended, for his own, for his uncle's, and even for his father's sake. In fact, Randolph appears to have been imprudent and unstable rather than dishonest, and may well have been the victim of High Federalist intrigues. Hamilton returned to the practice of law in order to maintain a steadily increasing family. Henry Knox, too, resigned; a good general, he had become "a furious Federalist" but an administrator of only modest capacity. By 1796 the government was completely re-cast; conscientious and combative Timothy Pickering at the State Department, the efficient and self-effacing Oliver Wolcott at the Treasury, the inefficient Irishman James McHenry as Secretary of War. New men—and by now an avowed principle. "I shall not", Washington wrote to Pickering, "whilst I have the honour to administer the government, bring a man into any office of consequence knowingly, whose political tenets are adverse to the measures which the general government are pursuing; for this, in my opinion, would be a sort of political suicide." Washington had come to a position he disliked and for which the Constitution gave no warrant; the pattern of party rivalry in the United States, like the pattern of government itself, stems from the years of his Administration.

The partisanship of the Press made Washington's last year in Philadelphia one of acute misery. He was particularly hurt by a reference of Jefferson's to the "men who were Samsons in the field and Solomons in the council, but who have had their heads shorn by the harlot England". He had, thundered the *Aurora*, "the ostentation of an eastern bashaw". He was alarmed at what, in his Farewell Address, he called "the banefull effects of the Spirit of Party"; the American people, he wrote in 1796, seemed "more disposed to promote the views of another nation than to establish a national character of their own"; he was being compared, he said, to a Nero, or even to a common pickpocket, after forty-five years of public service; he was tired of being "buffeted in the public prints by a set of infamous scribblers". His thoughts turned again to Addison's *Cato*—and to the idea of retirement.

The decision was not one of principle—though the refusal to consider a third term has subsequently become a hallowed convention, which all but one of his successors has honoured and which is now a Constitutional provision. But Washington was tired physically and mentally of the strains of office —and of the personal attacks. No one so sensitive about his "reputation" could long continue in a post now vulnerable to partisan attack, to innuendo and to public censure.

There has been much debate over the authorship of the Farewell Address (September 1796). Washington had always sought secretaries who, as he put it, would "possess the soul of the General"; though he left the writing of the Address to others, and especially to Hamilton, it incorporated—as he insisted it should—much of Madison's draft of 1792, and he went over it carefully himself. It is a Federalist document, the nearest approach in his writings to a declaration of the Washington *credo*. The unity of government he held to be primary; sectionalism and partisanship open the door "to foreign influence and corruption". More than anything else, Washington counselled against "the insidious wiles of foreign influence". It was not so much a policy of isolation from Europe that he advocated as the exclusion of Europe from America, and the maintenance thereby of an independent American national character. The "primary interests" of Europe and America were quite distinct. There should be no "permanent inveterate antipathies against particular nations, and passionate attachments for others", but constant vigilance, preparedness, and, if necessary, temporary alliances on extraordinary occasions.

Washington, though bequeathing a legacy and no doubt fully conscious of it, was also speaking in a particular situation, deploring the meddling of Genêt and Adet in American affairs, and the intrigues of Jefferson and Freneau, and advocating that the United States should have the strength to resist insults, whether from the Barbary pirates or the French revolutionaries or the captains of British frigates. He was speaking as a realist out of long experience, and concluded that nations, like men, must depend in the end on themselves alone—the lesson of all revolutions, the goal of all national movements. "There can be no greater error than to expect, or calculate upon real favours, from Nation to Nation." Not Isolation for all time, then, but Independence; not sectionalism or partisanship, though it appeared to be "inseparable from our nature", but loyalty to the national cause; not party controversy, but "strength and consistency" to give the country "the command of its own fortunes"; this was the legacy of 1776 as well as of 1796. Like all else he did, it set a precedent, and one of the wisest. The passing of the years has made Washington's Farewell Address almost as important a bequest of the first President as the drafting of the Constitution itself. It is read in both the Senate and the House of Representatives at noon on each 22nd February, as a tribute and as a reminder.

Washington's last speech to Congress was given on 7th December 1796. In it he pressed the case for a naval force, for a military academy and for a national university. It was dangerous, when revolution and war ravaged Europe, to send young Americans abroad at their most impressionable age. In a republic they should be taught "the science of government", and taught it at home. On 3rd March 1797, he presided at a dinner in honour of the President-elect, John Adams, and watched his inauguration on the following day. His diary is, as usual, laconic—"Much such a day as yesterday in all respects. Mercury at 41." The new President, who had not failed to criticise his predecessor, described the occasion to Abigail in more fulsome terms :

"A solemn scene it was indeed, and it was made more affecting to me by the presence of the General, whose countenance was as serene and unclouded as the day. He seemed to me to enjoy a triumph over me. Methought I heard him say 'Ay! I am fairly out and you fairly in'."

The role of Washington as President remains difficult to assess. It is clear that he began with a belief (shared by John Adams) in an independent executive, but that he moved steadily towards the Hamiltonians in his sympathies, especially after 1793; on financial matters he was completely dependent on Hamilton's guidance. Yet to the end Washington deplored the growth of parties; one reason he cited for refusing to consider a third term was that by 1796 party bitterness prevented universal acceptance of the President. The country would be no more united by him than by anyone else.

He does not appear as a very forceful leader in his own Administration : he provided few ideas; the problems that aroused him were those in which he had direct personal experience—relations with the Indians, military affairs, defence of the frontier, the maintenance of national unity. His Farewell Address says nothing about "the rights of man" and nothing about slavery, the basic threat to those rights in the next two generations; its theme is Washington's own even if the language is Hamilton's—the need for Union and the danger of foreign entanglements.

Beginning as a Head of State and hoping to remain above

faction, concerned to exalt the office of President and the authority of the new Government, Washington found that his Federalism itself rapidly generated partisanship. He was both hurt and baffled at the development, at the attacks of "the rascally Freneau", and at the savagery of Tom Paine's "Open Letter" from Paris in 1796. To use the language of an anonymous Philadelphia editor on the situation in 1788— "Thirteen staves and ne'er a hoop will not make a barrel." Washington sought to provide the hoop for the barrel. During his Presidency, five new states were added to the eleven that had accepted the Constitution : North Carolina (1789), Rhode Island (1790), Vermont (1791), Kentucky (1792) and Tennessee (1796). He moved away from a Virginian to a national, at times a nationalist, position; the break was not only with Jefferson, but with Madison, with Monroe and with Henry, despite the talk of nominating the last for Secretary of State in 1795. His system, he said, was to overlook all personal, local and partial considerations and "to contemplate the United States as one great whole".

Looking back, it appears surprising that Washington did not foresee the likelihood of the rise of party feeling. But Adams did not see it either, or if he did refused to face the consequences. He, too, tried to act as though the Executive were above party, representing the national interest, and paid the price in 1800. In Washington's case, the attitude is explicable enough. He was no theorist; his concern was with sound administration—of his estates, or of the Army, or of the nation. He could hardly be expected to know how bitter and irresponsible the Press charges would be, nor how savagely they would treat his concern with "respectability". "I was no party man myself", he wrote to Jefferson in 1796, "and the first wish of my heart was, if parties did exist, to reconcile them." What he did understand was the threat of sectionalism, and of States' Rights, to the unity won in 1783, and the threat of international revolution to the institutions of 1787. In this he was remarkably farsighted. He was the first leader of a successful national revolt against Imperialism in modern history, but for him, unlike Jefferson and Monroe and Paine, America's national revolt was not part of an international revolution. It was not part of a crusade to be launched across the world, but the product of a particular

situation in America in 1776. By 1797 the new and free
country had to be protected against revolution, as the constitution protected it against democracy. The America that
became the guide to Latin America in the 1820's, to Greece
and Hungary, Italy and Ireland, was Jefferson's not Washington's America.

The legacy of Washington's two terms was less political
than administrative. Washington was a gifted and experienced administrator, and the Federal Government, after
all, had fewer employees in 1790 than Mount Vernon. As
discipline was the soul of an army, so, he said, "system to
all things was the soul of business". System involved industry,
integrity, impartiality and firmness. "No man", said John
Adams, "has influence with the President. He seeks information from all quarters, and judges more independently than
any man I ever knew." His standards for appointments were
very high—higher than those in contemporary Britain or
France, higher than those of most of his successors. He
sought, and found, men who "would give dignity and lustre
to our National Character".

He was helped by rising prosperity. Though not an era of
good feelings, his Presidency was an era of good times. One
reason for the popularity of the Constitution was that it
coincided with this upswing. All sections of the nation and
all ranks of society shared in it, and the Federal government,
regardless of the party group in control, was the beneficiary.
In foreign affairs, too, Europe's ordeal was America's advantage; it produced settlement with Britain and Spain, it eased
the tension on the western border, and it made closer the
ties between the Tidewater and the trans-Allegheny country.
There were associated problems; the French Revolution gave
further impetus to American democracy, and foreign refugees and foreign ideas brought the risk of dangerous involvement in Europe. But in its prosperity at home and its
policy of peace abroad, the Washington Administration laid
a sound foundation for the new republic. Never before had
a republican government attempted to organise so vast an
area on a federal pattern. Rarely before had an executive
been so directly responsive to the popular assemblies. Rarely
has an office, that was to grow into the most important elec-

tive office in the world, been so clearly given the stamp of one man's character.

Washington sensed that Europe's distress could be for America destiny as well as advantage. "Sure I am", he wrote, "if this country is preserved in tranquillity twenty years longer, it may bid defiance in a just cause to any power whatever; such in that time will be its population, wealth and resources."

Chapter Nine

First Citizen: Last Years
(1797 — 1799)

WASHINGTON returned to Mount Vernon on 15th March 1797. Apart from one brief visit to Philadelphia, it was a return home for good. Farming and the administration of his own acres were for him the most satisfying of all activities, "innocent and useful". As he had written in 1788 to Arthur Young—"how much more delightful to the undebauched mind is the task of making improvements on the earth, than all the vain glory that can be acquired by ravaging it, by the most uninterrupted career of conquest". There were many jobs to be done, among them the erection of a house for his Papers, which, he thought, "are voluminous and may be interesting". He was surrounded by joiners and masons and painters; there was hardly a room "without the music of hammers or the odoriferous smell of paint". There were the familiar recurrent problems of driving the slaves to work, of ministering to them in illness, of planning the rotation of crops, of buying and selling.

In a letter to James McHenry, written in May, Washington has left a description of his round :

"I begin my diurnal course with the sun. . . . I examine the state of things further; and the more they are probed, the deeper I find the wounds are which my buildings have sustained by an absence and neglect of eight years; by the time I have accomplished these matters, breakfast (a little after seven o'clock, about the time I presume you are taking leave of Mrs. McHenry), is ready; . . . this being over, I mount my horse and ride round my farms, which employs me until it is time to dress for dinner, at which I rarely miss seeing strange faces, come as they say out of respect for me. Pray, would not the word curiosity answer as well? And how different this from having a few social friends at a cheerful board! The usual time of sitting at table, a walk, and tea, brings me within the dawn of candlelight; previous to which, if not prevented by company, I resolve, that, as soon as the glimmering taper supplies the place of the great luminary, I will retire to my writing-table and acknowledge the letters I have received; but when the lights are brought, I feel tired and disinclined to engage in this work, conceiving that the next night will do as well. The next comes, and with it the same causes for postponement and effect, and so on . . . I have not looked into a book since I came home; nor shall I be able to do it until I have discharged my workmen, probably not before the nights grow longer, when possibly I may be looking into Domesday Book."

The prospect of death never seemed far away now, and after 1795 there were many moods of depression, when he thought "the grim King would certainly master". Gilbert Stuart's numerous portraits make him appear rosy-cheeked and stalwart; though physically still a giant, in fact the years were leaving their mark on him. By 1796 his hair was very thin, his complexion sallow and all his teeth were gone. He was the proud possessor of two sets of awkward ivory false teeth, so ill-fitting that public speech was made more than ever difficult.

Yet Mount Vernon restored his health. He had his friends and family near him, particularly his step-granddaughter, Nellie Custis, and his nephew, Bushrod, who inherited Mount Vernon. When Nellie Custis described to him a Georgetown ball and said that none of the young men present had given her a moment's "uneasiness", he gave her wise and Polonius-like advice—"you, as others have done, may find perhaps that the passions of your sex are easier raised than allayed. Do not therefore boast too soon or too strongly of your unsensibility to, or resistance of, its power. In the composition of the human frame there is a good deal of inflammable matter. . . ."

It was shrewd advice, for on his birthday in February 1799 Nellie Custis married Washington's nephew Lawrence Lewis, and a daughter was born at Mount Vernon only two weeks before Washington died.

But it was not long before the country's crisis again disturbed the quiet of the lawns along the Potomac. France refused to accept C. C. Pinckney as American Minister in succession to Monroe; she threatened to apply to the United States the same regulations on neutral trade as the United States had accepted in the Jay Treaty; by June 1797 three hundred American ships and cargoes had been seized; and in October 1797 in the famous XYZ Affair, Talleyrand's agents, Hottingeur, Bellamy and Hauteval (or "XYZ"), implied that only bribery would permit the accredited agents of the American President to have access to the Directory. Pinckney's reply, "It is No, no, not a sixpence", has been transmuted by time into the classic "Millions for defence, but not one cent for tribute". Bribery was much more familiar a feature of eighteenth-century diplomacy in Europe than perhaps the good Americans realised—and bribery did not always involve money. John Marshall, one of the commissioners, and one of the first of American innocents abroad, seemed to be less impressed by XYZ than by a lady who accompanied them. But diplomatic discourtesy was one thing, humiliation was another. "I will never", said President Adams, "send another minister to France without assurance that he will be received, respected and honoured as the representative of a free, powerful and independent nation." A war spirit was provoked, and the Francophiles as well as the "Anglomen" were engulfed by it.

In this situation came another call to duty. A Navy Department was created, and 10,000 volunteers were to be raised for the Army. On 2nd July 1798, Adams nominated Washington as Commander-in-Chief; on the 3rd the Senate confirmed the nomination unanimously; on the 4th McHenry set off for Mount Vernon to concert plans. Washington agreed to serve, on condition that he need not move into the field until the Army needed him, and that he might have some share in the appointing of the General Staff. This produced tension—and, in fact, went far to split the Federalist party. For Washington wanted Hamilton as Inspector-General, virtually a Chief of Staff, and he had much support, including that of Pickering and McHenry. Adams, afraid of Washington's popularity and long hostile to Hamilton, favoured Knox, Pinckney and Hamilton as General Officers, and in that order, giving seniority as the excuse. The matter was not settled until October, in Hamilton's favour.

Knox refused to serve, and the most cordial and candid letters from Washington failed to win him over. Adams was angry, too, for he was convinced that Hamilton was "the most restless, impatient, artful, indefatigable and unprincipled intriguer in the United States". By 1798, and more clearly by 1800, there were Adams Federalists distinct from Hamiltonians, and the split gave victory in 1800 to the opposition. It was the beginning of government not only by party but by caucus.

The crisis of 1798 makes it clear that Washington by that time was not only a Hamiltonian but an avowed Nationalist. He saw in the Jeffersonians the enemies of his country, and the allies, perhaps the instruments, of foreign "wiles"— "you could as soon scrub the blackamore white as to change the principle of a profest Democrat . . . he will leave nothing uninterrupted to overturn the Government of this country". The distaste for the foreigner of 1778 was now explicit : "No foreigner will be admitted as a member of my family, while I retain my present ideas;—nor do I think they ought to be in any situation where they can come at secrets—and betray a trust." When the Alien and Sedition Acts were passed—empowering the President to deport or imprison "dangerous" aliens and making it a crime to attack the Government—Washington supported them without hesitation.

He made the same points in letters, especially to Lafayette. He deplored what he thought the intrigues of the French to set the American people against their own government; if they wanted accommodation, let them evidence it by action, "for words unaccompanied therewith will not be much regarded now". The government and people "are truly Americans in principle . . . France . . . is interfering in the internal concerns of all nations, neutral as well as belligerent, and setting the world in an uproar". "My politics", he told his old friend of 1778, "are plain and simple. I think every nation has a right to establish that form of government, under which it conceives it shall live most happy; provided it infracts no right, or is not dangerous to others." The language of 1798 is not unfamiliar; it, too, expresses a persistent thread in American foreign policy, and recurs in 1850, in 1917-18 and in 1949.

In 1798 and 1799 an undeclared war was fought at sea; war fever mounted, fostered by Hamilton, deplored by Adams. In February 1799, to the universal surprise, the President nominated William Vans Murray as Minister to France, assuring the Senate that Murray would not, in fact, depart for Paris until he had received an assurance that he would be honourably received. The Hamiltonians were indignant and added two other names to the commission. In October 1799, Adams took the courageous step of authorising the commissioners to sail. By the time they reached Paris, there was a new star in the ascendant there and settlement was not difficult.

The situation of 1798 was not only a war crisis. It was a clash of two men and two attitudes inside the Federalist party. Washington had become in some degree the symbol of the country's cause, for influence over whom Hamilton and Adams were contending. Hamilton won the battle for influence; Adams won the campaign, by daring to keep the peace with France in face of a wave of jingoism. Washington was no longer master of this factional situation. He was worried by the Kentucky Resolutions, the Jeffersonian reply to the Alien and Sedition Acts, the first whisper of secession; he was worried by the conditions in the West, and pleaded for an army engineer to plan its defences. There must be a "national design" in them; the man himself—and it was a lot to ask in the Mississippi country in 1799—must be "attached to the true policy and interest of the United States". This was now his dominant theme.

As the war clouds gathered and the Federalists were divided, Washington's name was talked of again for President. He refused to entertain the idea: he would not draw, he said, a single vote from the Jeffersonians; any other "respectable Federal character would receive the same suffrages". Again he was ready to serve, and there was no democratic talk of one, two or three terms. What swayed him at the end as throughout his life was prudence—and reputation: "I should become a mark for the shafts of envenomed malice . . . I should be charged not only with irresolution but with concealed ambition . . . with dotage and imbecility." And by

1799 he was tired. "A mind that has been constantly on the stretch since the year 1753, with but short intervals and little relaxation, requires rest and composure."

His friends had commented on his fitness in 1797, after the return to Mount Vernon. The strain of 1798, however, affected his health. A bout of fever in August 1799 was slow to clear, and left him weak.

On 12th December 1799 he rode around his farms from mid-morning to mid-afternoon, on his usual inspection. But snow was falling steadily, the wind was icy, and on his return his secretary, Tobias Lear, noticed snow on his hair and moisture on his neck. He sat down to dinner without changing his damp clothes. The next day he complained of a sore throat and a chill. During the night he grew worse and was breathing with difficulty. The doctors who were summoned, including his old comrade Dr. Craik, resorted to the barbarous and blundering recourse of the century—he was bled four times, and as a result grew steadily weaker. As in Molière's day, it was still true that men were dying of their remedies rather than of their diseases.

Washington seems to have thought from the beginning that his illness was likely to be fatal. "Doctor," he said to Craik, "I die hard but I am not afraid to go." In the afternoon he gave instructions about his will. By nightfall, the pain had increased, swallowing was impossible, and he was exhausted by the swelling in his throat, by laxatives and emetics and by bloodletting. Just before his death, the faithful group around him, of doctors, Martha, Lear and his negro house-servant Christopher, saw him put the fingers of his left hand on his right wrist and saw his lips move as he tried to count his pulse. Washington died about ten o'clock on the evening of 14th December 1799. Four days later, after a simple ceremony, he was interred in the plain vault on the hillside at Mount Vernon. Martha died two and a half years later.

Chapter Ten

"Dr. The United States . . . in Account with—G: Washington Cr."

DESPITE the criticism of the Jeffersonians, the legend grew, even before Washington's death. The "Federal City" soon became "Washington". On the centenary of his First Inaugural, a state was given his name, admitted as the forty-second to the still growing and ever more powerful Union. By this time counties and towns and mountains are called after him, and his home is a national shrine. He has been immortalised in literature, honoured as General, as Founding Father and as architect of government.

The monument to honour him had, however, a chequered history. Its erection was delayed by the Civil War and the aftermath of Reconstruction, by the years when Washington's State led the War against Washington's Union, and when both Lee and Lincoln invoked his name. It was finally completed in 1884, a single shaft, marble without, granite within, rising five hundred and fifty feet above the ground. It gives a commanding view of the Federal City : to the north, the White House, not yet completed in 1799, and beyond, in Lafayette Square, the statues to those from foreign lands who came to play their part in the American Revolution—Lafayette and Rochambeau, Kosciusko and von Steuben; to the east, the Capitol, to the west the Lincoln Memorial, and to the south, across the tidal basin, the rotunda to honour Jefferson. In the western distance is the haze of the Blue Ridge, and, fifteen miles away, south-west down the Potomac, is Mount Vernon, which Washington inherited and farmed and loved. The Washington Monument has not the grace of the Jefferson Memorial, framed by drifts of cherry and dogwood; there are no queues of negro children as at the Lincoln Memorial, visiting the shrine of the Emancipator; but it serves to recall those virtues, simple and rare, which denigrators and hagiographers alike have seen in him—integrity, circumspection, dignity, constancy.

These sober abstractions do little to convey the force and fire of the man; he appears temperate in spirit when in fact he was tempered by great events. But they are the qualities that are associated with practical success. Washington's career was astonishingly successful—as surveyor, explorer and planter, in his choice of a wife, as leader of a rebellion, as organiser of a government. No other figure in American history has the stature of Washington, not merely because he was Commander of the Revolutionary Army and the first President, but because no other figure can expect to have his degree of success. Lee, who rivals him as a Virginian gentleman and took him as an example in 1861, has the aura of the Southern cause about him, and the magic and romance of failure. His is the story of ill-fortune nobly borne and of the triumph of character over catastrophe. It has been said, as a result, that "Virginia admires Washington but worships Lee", that Lee was "Washington without his reward". Lincoln, whose folksy manner and background are completely remote from the ordered world of the eighteenth-century planters, is made heroic not only by his achievements but by the drama of his martyrdom. Had he lived through Reconstruction it seems safe to assume that he would have met criticism at least as savage as that visited on Washington. The mistakes both Lee and Lincoln made are dwarfed by the contrast with the bigger tragedies of their lives; in the light of the tragedy of the Civil War both men appear more than life-size, the great patrician and the great democrat.

Washington's success is a tale of a different sort, a triumph of the unheroic qualities, of planning, detail and application, blessed by a good fortune that failed to smile on Lincoln or on Lee.

This is not to say that the success was unqualified : there were errors in tactics in the war, minimised by later historians —like the campaign in New York, and even the choice of Valley Forge as a winter camp; there was a caution in committing himself to the Constitutional Convention that shows more calculation than courage, more prudence than statesmanship; there was at the end a partisanship in domestic matters that suggests that the President was either bewildered by the problems facing him or thoroughly exhausted. And success, if carefully manufactured and too laboriously gained —the preoccupation with "honour", "reputation" and "approbation", the marshalling and revision of the State Papers at Mount Vernon, the bridling under criticism—can be won at a heavy price. But these flaws, if they are such, are undramatic and do not affect the main canvas.

Nor is Washington's reputation affected by his indifference to some searching contemporary problems. Like many of his friends, Washington regretted that he had slaves—"I do not like even to think, much less talk of it." But his attitude was that of the practical man; his letters reveal a firm master who expected his slaves to do their full share of work, and who was ready when he sold them to "brighten them up" a little. His criticism of the institution of slavery was that it was uneconomic rather than that it was immoral. He expressed himself in favour of gradual abolition—the prevailing sentiment of his time—and left instructions in his will that his slaves should be freed at the death of his wife and a trust fund set up for them; but for the most part his views were those of the property owner not of the reformer.

So it was with religion. There are few references to it in his letters, though many to Providence and destiny. He believed in religion as a pillar of society—witness his Farewell Address—and he had been a good vestryman and church attender in Virginia; but this was largely social formality. When Dr. Abercrombie, his pastor in Philadelphia, criticised him as President for not taking communion, he never went again on communion Sundays. Bishop White said that he had never seen Washington kneel at prayer. No minister of religion was summoned to the bedside as he lay dying. Moral and spiritual issues had much less meaning for him than for his great Virginian contemporary.

His contribution was of another kind. The physical capacity of the man, the extent of his travels through the new country, the range of his experience, his knowledge of the West, as well as of South and North—these brought unique qualities to deal with the complex issues of 1776, 1787 and 1789. His increasing concern with the Federal

cause, the reiteration in his later letters of the words
"American" and "national", the balance and discretion with
which he walked in the years after 1787, the wisdom of his
decisions on the main questions, the immense success of the
precedents he set, his own very human pride in himself and
in the office of President—these are Washington's abiding
claims to the respect and admiration of his countrymen. It
was his practical achievement and his integrity that earned
him Henry Lee's tribute of being "first in War, first in peace
and first in the hearts of his countrymen". "Our history is
but a transcript of his claims on our gratitude", orated Fisher
Ames. "Our nation shares with him the singular glory of
having conducted a civil war with mildness and a revolution with order."

As the years have passed, the clouds have hidden the
mountain top. In the last generation some of Washington's
biographers have sought to find again the man inside the
myth, to discover the "real" Washington. At this point in
time, it is probably an impossible task; it is nearly a century
since it was said that if Washington returned to life and
stood alongside his portraits and was seen not to resemble
them, he would be called the impostor.

The quest for the "historical" Washington in any event
makes a false distinction. Private life in eighteenth-century
Virginia was lived publicly; one's character was known all
too clearly by one's most ruthless critics, the neighbours.
Franklin described it as a society where "He who drinks his
wine alone, can catch his horse alone". Washington con-
formed to this social and hospitable Virginian code. The
diaries from 1768 until his election as Commander-in-Chief
in 1775—the only revealing account of his years as a private
citizen—show him particularly fond of fox-hunting, of dancing and of cards. These were the amusements of his class,
but they were not part of a class system. There was no
Mount Vernon "hunt", no special costume or style. Washington raised his own pack, bred his own horses, broke them
himself to the saddle. The sport was a home product, and all
friends and neighbours who cared were welcome to join in.
In these seven and a half years, he spent 1,885 days at Mount
Vernon, and in this period he had 1,988 guests, four-fifths of
whom stayed to dinner or over-night—little groups stayed

longer from two days to two weeks. The house was not as large as it is now, and this burden on Martha and himself was considerable. But it was borne without question, for it was the general Virginian practice.

In this society, conduct mattered most, and Washington's life was untouched by scandal or rumour. Nor in a plantation economy could private life be divorced from public office. The striking feature of Washington's years as soldier and as President is the extent of the identity of his own career with his country's cause. To study his life is to study his country's history—and to appreciate the single-mindedness that was the product of the planter's code. In attempting to penetrate to the man behind the myth, it is not necessary, therefore, to postulate, as some recent biographers have done, that he was different from what he seemed, that he was "really" complex and involved. Washington was fortunate in his simplicity and in his straightforwardness; his gift of silence may have given depth and a sense of mystery to his personality, but it was not hiding anything. It has, however, helped to establish him, God-like and anaconic, in the popular imagination.

This is not to pretend that Washington never told a lie, that he sank on his knees at prayer in the snow at Valley Forge or to accept the embroideries of Parson Weems and other patriotic diggers. The capacity to provide material for national mythology is not the least of Washington's services. "The Man", says Carlyle, "is the spirit he worked in; not what he did, but what he became."

When irascible John Adams said of him that "The Great Character was a Character of Convention", he failed to appreciate the significance of the phrase. Behind the conventions there were stored up here all the symbols necessary for legends. There were dignity and style, captured in stone and on canvas by Houdon, Stuart and the Peale family, and evidenced by his taste for a coach and crests and outriders in attendance; there was an Olympian aloofness, the manner of an Eastern monarch rather than a republican general, as though dedicated to the leadership of the new nation from the beginning—no children of his own, it has been said, the better to allow him to be the *Pater Patriæ*. "Not a King in Europe", said a London newspaper, "but would look like a *valet de chambre* by his side." There was, too, the success story, of the raw-boned youth of no particular education, selfish for land and for reputation, who became the wealthiest land-owner of his generation, the master of 60,000 acres and 300 slaves, the most dignified of gentlemen, the most honoured of Americans at home and abroad. There are the paradoxes, of the Tidewater planter who knew the rough and unmapped frontier at first hand; of the aristocrat —"Take none but gentlemen"—who became the leader of the democratic cause that he only dimly understood; of the business-man who was too proud to serve for pay but not too proud to fight, who indeed in carrying on the fight kept alive the cause; of the man of caution who could finally put his courage and his reputation to the sticking-point, in war, in political debate and then in government, and prove successful in all three; of the Virginian who became "American", but whose first thoughts were always of Mount Vernon and of the "Northern Neck", his lands and his horses, a figure at once parochial and patriarchal. There is the Roman republican, the farmer-turned-soldier and the farmer-turned-President, uncorrupted by nepotism and untempted by power, respectful of the civil authority and of the people's will. Not least there was the rare capacity to endure misfortune, an inability, almost, to recognise disaster when he met it. These qualities, like the concern with status, the composure and the lack of introspection, are again Roman and republican : *constantia et gravitas*. To be First Citizen was for Washington the final tribute, whereas for the other great contemporary leader of revolutionary armies, to be First Consul was the beginning of a career of conquest. It was important for his country's future that the first of the Presidents should have the "Character of Convention".

A fellow-Virginian shall have the last word. Perceptive and compassionate, Thomas Jefferson wrote of Washington in 1814 :

"His mind was great and powerful, without being of the very first order; his penetration strong, though not so acute as that of a Newton, Bacon, or Locke; and as far as he saw, no judgment was ever sounder. It was slow in operation, being little aided by invention or imagination, but sure in conclusion. Hence the common remark of his officers, of the advantage he derived from councils of war, where hearing all suggestions, he selected whatever was best; and certainly no General ever planned his battles more judiciously. But if deranged during the course of the action, if any member of his plan was dislocated by sudden circumstances, he was slow in readjustment. The consequence was, that he often failed in the field, and rarely against an enemy in station, as at Boston and York.

"He was incapable of fear, meeting personal dangers with the calmest unconcern. Perhaps the strongest feature in his character was prudence, never acting until every circumstance, every consideration, was maturely weighed; refraining if he saw a doubt, but, when once decided going through with his purpose, whatever obstacles opposed. His integrity was most pure, his justice the most inflexible I have ever known, no motives of interest or consanguinity, of friendship or hatred, being able to bias his decision. He was, indeed, in every sense of the words, a wise, a good, and a great man.

"His temper was naturally high toned; but reflection and resolution had obtained a firm and habitual ascendency over it. If ever, however, it broke its bonds, he was most tremendous in his wrath. In his expenses he was honorable, but exact; liberal in contributions to whatever promised utility; but frowning and unyielding on all visionary projects and all unworthy calls on his charity. His heart was not warm in its affections; but he exactly calculated every man's value, and gave him a solid esteem proportioned to it. His person, you know, was fine, his stature exactly what one would wish, his deportment easy, erect and noble; the best horseman of his age, and the most graceful figure that could be seen on horseback. Although in the circle of his friends, where he might be unreserved with safety, he took a free share in conversation, his colloquial talents were not above mediocrity, possessing neither copiousness of ideas, nor fluency of words. In public, when called on for a sudden opinion, he was unready, short and embarrassed. Yet he wrote readily, rather diffusely, in an easy and correct style. This he had acquired by conversation with the world, for his education was merely reading, writing, and common arithmetic, to which he added surveying at a later day.

"His time was employed in action chiefly, reading little, and that only in agriculture and English history. His correspondence became necessarily extensive, and, with journalizing his agricultural proceedings, occupied most of his leisure hours within doors.

"On the whole, his character was, in its mass, perfect, in nothing bad, in few points indifferent; and it may truly be said, that never did nature and fortune combine more perfectly to make a man great, and to place him in the same constellation with whatever worthies have merited from man an everlasting remembrance. For his was the singular destiny and merit, of leading the armies of his country successfully through an arduous war, for the establishment of its independence; of conducting its councils through the birth of a government, new in its forms and principles, until it had settled down into a quiet and orderly train; and of scrupulously obeying the laws through the whole of his career, civil and military, of which the history of the world furnishes no other example."

A Note on Books

THE literature on Washington and his times is enormous. Some delightful contemporary sources for eighteenth-century Virginia have recently been made available : Robert Beverley's *The History and Present State of Virginia*, published in London, 1705 (edited by Louis B. Wright for the Institute of Early American History and Culture at Williamsburg, Virginia, 1947), *The Secret Diary of William Byrd of Westover, 1709-12* (edited by L. B. Wright and M. Tinling and published by the Dietz Press in Richmond in 1941) and *The Journal and Letters of Philip Vickers Fithian, 1773-1774: A Plantation Tutor of the Old Dominion* (edited by H. D. Farish and published by Colonial Williamsburg, Inc., in 1943). Extracts from these and other contemporary writings can be found in *Virginia Reader, a treasury of writings from the first voyages to the present*, edited by Francis Coleman Rosenberger in 1948 (E. P. Dutton, New York, 1948). In 1953 the Tracy McGregor Library of the University of Virginia published Richard Oswald's Memorandum of 1781 *On the Folly of invading Virginia* (ed. by W. Stitt Robinson Jr.). In *America Rebels: Narratives of the Patriots* (Pantheon Books, New York, 1953), R. M. Dorson prints some interesting eye-witness accounts of the Revolution.

For one who is not customarily regarded as an author, Washington left an immense body of writing : John C. Fitzpatrick collected thirty-nine volumes for the Bicentennial Commission in 1931 (1931-44), and he has also edited, in four volumes, Washington's very unrevealing *Diaries* (1925). Saxe Commins (*Basic Writings of George Washington*, Random House, 1948) and Saul Padover (*The Washington Papers*, Harper's, 1954) have each produced single-volume collections. The classic contemporary analysis of the Constitution is *The Federalist* (edited by Max Beloff in Blackwell's Political Texts in 1948).

Biographies of Washington are legion, from the early

hagiography of "Parson" Weems (1800) and of John Marshall (1805–7) down to the more critical assessments of the last twenty years. The best, the most detailed, but, unhappily, an uncompleted study, is Douglas Southall Freeman's, in six volumes (1948–53). There are briefer biographies by Rupert Hughes, three volumes (1926–30; critical), W. E. Woodward (1926; debunking), Stephenson and Dunn, two volumes (1940; laudatory) and Bernhard Knollenberg (1940; critical and stimulating on Washington as commander). The best studies of the West in Washington's time are by C. H. Ambler, *George Washington and the West* (1936) and T. P. Abernethy, *Western Lands and the American Revolution* (1937).

Of more general books on the Revolutionary period, reference might be made to John C. Miller, *The Origins of the American Revolution* (1943), and his *Triumph of Freedom, 1775–1783* (1948), and E. B. Greene, *The Revolutionary Generation, 1763–90* (1943, in the History of American Life Series). New light is thrown on the causes of the Revolution by Philip Davidson, *Propaganda and the American Revolution* (1941), by L. A. Harper, *English Navigation Laws* (1939), by O. M. Dickerson, *The Navigation Acts and the American Revolution* (1951) and by Elisha P. Douglass, *Rebels and Democrats* (1955).

Older studies still worth attention include Charles Beard's classic *Economic Interpretation of the Constitution* (1913), J. F. Jameson's *The American Revolution Considered as a Social Movement* (1926) and A. M. Schlesinger, senior, *The Colonial Merchants and the American Revolution* (1918). On the Confederation period, older works have been displaced by Merrill Jensen, *The New Nation: A History of the United States During the Confederation, 1781–1789* (1950). Carl Van Doren, *The Great Rehearsal* (1948) is a vivid picture of the Constitution-making. There are revisionary estimates of Beard's interpretation in Irving Brant's life of *Madison* (1941–), five volumes to date; in W. W. Crosskey, *Politics and the Constitution* (1953), two volumes, and in Daniel Boorstin, *The Genius of American Politics* (1953). The best recent study of the Washington Administration is L. D. White, *The Federalists* (1948).

Index

INDEX